TEACHER'S GUIDE

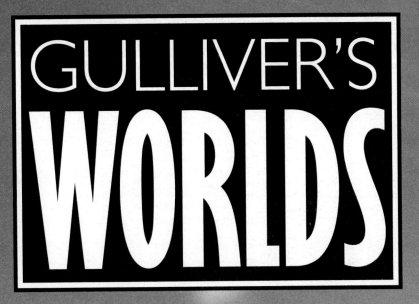

GULLIVER'S WORLDS

MEASURING AND SCALING

MathScape™
Seeing and Thinking
Mathematically

The *McGraw·Hill* Companies

Send all inquiries to:
Glencoe/McGraw-Hill
8787 Orion Place
Columbus, OH 43240-4027

ISBN: 0-07-866803-4

4 5 6 079 08 07 06

Glencoe

New York, New York
Columbus, Ohio
Chicago, Illinois
Peoria, Illinois
Woodland Hills, California

Education Development Center, Inc.

Curriculum Developers for *Gulliver's Worlds*
Glenn Kleiman

EDC Project Director
Glenn Kleiman

EDC Core Staff
Amy Brodesky, Rebecca Brown, Dan Brutlag, Emily Fagan, Kristen Herbert, Shelley Isaacson, Susan Janssen, Kathryn Rasala, Stacy Shorr, Yael Sucher, Andrea Tench, Dan Tobin, Karen Zweig

Other EDC Contributors
Al Cuoco, E Paul Goldenberg, Marlene Kliman, Leigh Peake, Sue Rasala, Faye Ruopp, Kimberly Smart, Ellen Smith, Marianne Thompson, Albertha Walley, Muffie Wiebe

Additional Contributors
Kristen Bjork, Cindy Char, Stacie Cassat, Stephen Krinsky, Joan Miceli, Michael Peller

Project Collaborators & Consultants
EdMath: Charles Lovitt, Doug Clarke, Ian Lowe

Shell Centre for Mathematical Education: Hugh Burkhardt, Rosemary Caddy, Malcolm Swan

ACKNOWLEDGMENTS

 ## MathScape Background

The STM project built upon EDC's 40-year history of developing educational materials, including PSSC Physics, ESS Science, The Infinity Factory television series, Insights Science, The Geometric Supposer software series, My Travels with Gulliver, and many other curriculum, software, and video products.

This unit is one of a series of twenty-one MathScape: Seeing and Thinking Mathematically units designed to fully address current standards and recommendations for teaching middle school mathematics. The Seeing and Thinking Mathematically project involved international collaboration with:

- The Shell Centre for Mathematical Education at the University of Nottingham, England, whose contributions built upon many years of research and development underlying materials such as The Language of Functions and Graphs.

- EdMath of Victoria, Australia, whose staff built upon years of research and development producing materials such as the Mathematics Curriculum and Teaching Program (MCTP) materials.

- Inverness Research Associates of California provided consulting on the design of the research processes used in the project and conducted research for several of the units.

The Seeing and Thinking Mathematically project incorporated many formative research activities to assist the developers in designing materials that are mathematically clear and pedagogically effective with diverse populations of students. These activities included summer institutes with middle school teachers, consultations with experts on teaching mathematics to students from different cultural and linguistic backgrounds, reviews of the research on children's learning of mathematics, input from many consultants and advisors, and classroom testing of activities in which the project staff and teachers worked closely together. These research activities helped to define the design principles used throughout the curriculum.

Building from the design principles, initial versions of each unit were then carefully tested in a variety of classrooms, ensuring feedback from multiple teachers and diverse groups of students. Project researchers conducted weekly classroom observations and teacher interviews. Student work was collected and analyzed to evaluate the lessons and identify common student misconceptions. The project researchers and curriculum developers used this extensive field test data to revise and improve the units. The field test teachers' classroom experiences and suggestions were also incorporated into the final units in the form of "From the Classrooms" and "A Teacher Reflects."

MathScape: Seeing and Thinking Mathematically was developed by the Seeing and Thinking Mathematically project (STM), based at Education Development Center, Inc. (EDC), a non-profit educational research and development organization in Newton, MA. The STM project was supported, in part, by the National Science Foundation Grant No. 9054677. Opinions expressed are those of the authors and not necessarily those of the Foundation.

Credits

Teacher's Guide Credits::
All photography by
Chris Conroy.

Student Guide Credits:
All photography by
Chris Conroy.

Field Test Teachers

We wish to extend special thanks to the following teachers and their students for their roles in field testing and reviewing units developed by EDC.

ARLINGTON, MA
Carol Martignette
 Boswell
Steve Porretta

BELMONT, MA
Tony Guarante
Heidi Johnson

BOSTON, MA
Patricia Jorsling
George Perry
Elizabeth Prieto
Bill Rudder

BROOKLINE, MA
Robert Bates
Frank Cabezas
Carolyn Connolly
Arlene Geller-Petrini
Sandra Hegsted
Oakley Hoerth
Judy McCarthy
Carol Mellet
Fran Ostrander
Barabara Scotto
Rhonda Weinstein

Debbie Winkler
Deanna Wong

CAMBRIDGE, MA
Mary Lou Mehring
Jennie Schmidt
Jesse Solomon

FREMONT, CA
Julie Dunkle

INDIO, CA
Lisa Sullivan

LAKEVIEW, CA
Jane Fesler

MILL VALLEY, CA
Patty Armstrong

NEW CANAAN, CT
Sue Kelsey
Bruce Lemoine

NEWTON, MA
Sonya Grodberg
David Lawrence
Mark Rubel

SAN FRANCISCO, CA
Andrianna Gualco
Ingrid Oyen

SOMERVILLE, MA
Jean Foley

**SOUTH SAN
FRANCISCO, CA**
Doug Harik

SUDBURY, MA
Fred Gross
Sondra Hamilton
Jackie Simms

TEMECULA, CA
Ray Segal

TIBURON, CA
Julie Askeland

WALTHAM, MA
Amy Doherty
Diane Krueger
Pat Maloney

We extend our appreciation to Judy Mumme and the following teachers and educators involved in the California Middle School Mathematics Renaissance Project.

Cathy Carroll
SAN MATEO, CA

Deb Clay
HUNTINGTON BEACH, CA

Kathryn Conley
MERCED, CA

Joan Easterday
SANTA ROSA, CA

Linda Fisher
SANTA CRUZ, CA

Marty Hartrick
SAN FRANCISCO, CA

Kevin Jordan
CARMEL, CA

Steve Leliever
LONG BEACH, CA

Carole Maples
WALNUT CREEK, CA

Guillermo Mendieta
AZUSA, CA

Teferi Messert
SACRAMENTO, CA

Mark Rubell
NEWTON, CA

Charles Schindler
RUNNING SPRINGS, CA

Aminah Talib
CARSON, CA

Kevin Truitt
LOS ANGELES, CA

Classroom Testing Teachers

Our thanks to the following classroom teachers for their contributions on the MathScape units.

Bev Brockhoff
Geoff Burroughs
Linda Carmen
Janet Casagrande
Karen Chamberlin
Laura Chan
April Cherrington
Marian Connelly
Barbara Creedon
Kathy Duane
Jennifer Dunmire
Karen Edmonds
Sara Effenbeck
John Friedrich
Lisa Gonzales
Andrianna Gualco
Doug Harik
Jennifer Hoggarty
Lynn Hoggatt
Judy Jones
Sue Lackey
Joan LaComb
Stan Lake
Amanda LaRocca
Claudia Larson
Mona Lasley
Maria Majka

Jim McHugh
Fernando Mendez
Michael Merk
Carol Moore
John Mulkerrins
John Osness
Charles Perez
Dave Peters
Linda Peters
Lisa Phillips
Jim Pinckard
Mark Ristow
Thelma Rodriguez
Ellen Ron
Emiliano Sanchez
Janet Schwarz
Cindi Sekera
Doris Seldon
Gale Sunderland
Jim Tearpak
Barbara Termaat
Brenda Walker
David Ward
Brenda Watson
Howard Web
Nancy Withers
Hanne Young

TABLE OF

GULLIVER'S WORLDS

Measuring and Scaling

This unit, inspired by the classic story *Gulliver's Travels,* allows students to link literature, writing, and mathematics. By following Gulliver's adventures as recorded in journal entries, students learn about measurement, estimation, computation, scale, proportion, area, and volume.

PHASE ONE

Brobdingnag

Students use measurement and estimation to determine the scale factor that relates the sizes of things in mythical Brobdingnag to the sizes of things in real-life Ourland.

PHASE TWO

Lilliput

Students use measurement, estimation, and clues from Gulliver's journal to determine the scale factor—this time one that reduces the sizes of objects. They explore the effect of rescaling on linear, area, and volume measures.

CONTENTS

Additional UNIT RESOURCES

Quick Review Math Handbook

MathScape™ is supported by Glencoe's *Quick Review Math Handbook,* also known as *hot* **words**™, *hot* **topics**™. The handbook contains a glossary, how-to information, and problems for additional homework and practice.

The *hot* **words**™ that appear on the lesson pages in the Student Guide are mathematical terms related to the lesson.

hot **topics**™ The *hot* **topics**™ appearing in the Teacher's Guide indicate mathematical topics that are recommended for optional review and homework.

If your students do not have the *hot* **words**™, *hot* **topics**™ handbook, you can use the *hot* **words**™ for discussion, referencing them in any mathematical glossary or dictionary. You can use the recommended *hot* **topics**™ as a guide to help you organize review material.

MathScape™ Online

Visit **www.mathscape1.com** for the following tools:

- Online Study Tools
- Technology Options
- Curriculum Links
- Teacher Reflections
- Bulletin Board

Print Components

Math Skills Maintenance Masters

Use the Math Skills Maintenance Masters to keep your students' basic math skills fresh. Students can review skills one at a time or in a combined format.

Investigations for the Special Education Student in the Mathematics Classroom

Use the long-term investigations in this booklet with your special education students. Each investigation includes a list of ways in which the activities may be adapted or modified depending on the student population of the class.

Investigation Number	Title
10	Taste Test
14	Park It!
24	Explore the Depths of the Sea

Technology Components

The CD-ROM includes a lesson planner and interactive Teacher's Guide, so you can customize lesson plans and reproduce classroom resources quickly and easily.

StudentWorks

This backpack solution CD-ROM allows students instant access to the Student Guide and reproducible pages.

ExamView Pro

Use the networkable testmaker to:
- create multiple versions of tests,
- create modified tests for inclusion students,
- edit existing questions, and
- add your own questions.

VirtualActivities

Use the following Virtual Activities for individual, small group, or whole-class instruction. This CD-ROM connects the following mathematics concepts to real-world situations.
- The Metric System
- Line Symmetry

What's MATH Got To Do With It? Real-Life Math Videos

Level 1, Video 4 Use *Chimpanzees and School Lunches* to engage your students in real-world situations involving ratio, proportion, and percent.

Things You Should KNOW

The Teacher's Guide contains complete lesson plans, assessment, and reproducible pages. Look for these icons to help you make the most of the Teacher's Guide.

This icon identifies **notes** of special interest within the teaching steps. These notes often include an indication of what to expect from student writing or discussions.

This icon identifies **comments** from teachers who have used this unit in the classroom. Their experiences and practical suggestions appear in the margin of the Teacher's Guide.

A reduced version of the **Student Guide** page is shown in the Teacher's Guide for easy reference. The arrow icon is used to indicate that the notes on the Teacher's Guide page correspond directly to the Student Guide page.

June 20th, 1702

I, Lemuel Gulliver, hereby begin a journal of my adventures. This will not be a complete record, for I am not by nature the most faithful of writers. I do promise, however, to include any and all events of general interest.

The urge to visit strange and exotic lands has driven me since my youth, when I studied medicine in London. I often spent my spare time learning navigation and other parts of mathematics useful to travelers.

This spring I shipped out in the ship named Adventure under Captain John Nicholas. I had signed on as ship's doctor, and we were bound for Surat. We had a good voyage until we passed the Straits of Madagascar. There the winds blew strongly, and continued for the next twenty days. We were carried fifteen hundred miles to the east, farther than the oldest sailor aboard had ever been.

Lemuel Gulliver

How big are things in Gulliver's Worlds?

GULLIVER'S WORLDS

UNIT OVERVIEW

Introduction
How big are things in Gulliver's Worlds?

Stranded in a land of giants, Gulliver must discover the scale of things to understand this new world and learn to live in it. In the classic story *Gulliver's Travels,* author Jonathan Swift accurately portrays each detail in the story using mathematics. Because he describes not only Gulliver's height in relation to the Lilliputians, but also compares the area of his footprint and the volume of Lilliputian food Gulliver would need to survive, Swift is able to create three-dimensional worlds of giants and tiny people.

In this unit, students link literature, writing, and mathematics as they step into *Gulliver's Worlds.* The story of Gulliver's adventures, told through journal entries, leads students to learn more about measurement, estimation, computation, scale, proportion, area, and volume. Students apply these concepts as they create their own stories, artifacts, and displays about *Gulliver's Worlds.*

Curriculum Links

This unit can be part of an interdisciplinary unit on size. There are many folktales that focus on tiny or giant people or people who change sizes. These can be used in mathematical activities where students determine a scale factor in a story. The following books and materials will help students link mathematics to other curriculum topics.

Books

The Indian in the Cupboard, by Lynne R. Banks

The Mysterious Giant of Barletta, by Tomie DePaola

Powers of Ten: A Book About the Relative Size of Things in the Universe and the Effect of Adding Another Zero, by Philip Morrison

The Shrinking of Treehorn, by F. P. Heide

Online Research

The following words can be used as starting points for online research.

- size
- giant
- scale
- Gulliver

MathScape™ Online

The Jaffe Gulliver Site is an interactive Web site filled with images and excellent online links, plus an edited, formatted version of the complete text of *Gulliver's Travels.* To learn more, visit:

www.mathscape1.com/curriculumlinks

PHASE**ONE**
Brobdingnag

Gulliver's journal holds clues to sizes of things in Brobdingnag, a land of giants. Using these clues, you will find ways to predict the sizes of other things. Then you will use math to create a life-size drawing of a giant object. You will also compare sizes in the two lands. Finally, you will use what you know about scale to write a story set in Brobdingnag.

PHASE**TWO**
Lilliput

Lilliput is a land of tiny people. Gulliver's journal and drawings will help you find out about the sizes of things in Lilliput. You will compare the measurement system in Lilliput to ours. Then you will explore area and volume as you figure out how many Lilliputian objects are needed to feed and house Gulliver. Finally, you will write a story set in Lilliput.

PHASE**THREE**
Lands of the Large and Lands of the Little

Clues from pictures will help you write a scale factor that relates the sizes of things in different lands to the sizes of things in Ourland. You will continue to explore length, area, and volume, and see how these measures change as the scale changes. Finally, you will put together all you have learned to create a museum exhibit about one of these lands.

AT A GLANCE

PHASE ONE
Brobdingnag

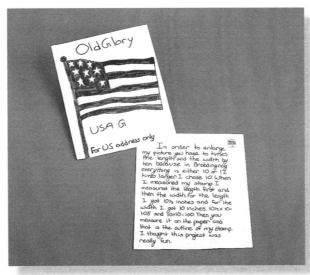

As students read Gulliver's journal entries from Brobdingnag, the land of giants, they use measurement and estimation to determine the scale factor that relates the sizes of things in Brobdingnag to the sizes of things in Ourland, the land where we live. Students use this scale factor to make life-size drawings of objects from Brobdingnag. They compare the sizes of objects in Brobdingnag to those in Ourland, and explore area and volume relationships to solve various problems. At the end of the phase, students demonstrate their understanding of scale by writing a mathematically accurate story set in Brobdingnag.

PHASE TWO
Lilliput

Students continue reading Gulliver's journal as he moves on to Lilliput, the land of tiny people. Again, they use measurement, estimation, and clues from the journal to determine the scale factor—this time one that reduces the sizes of objects. They create actual-size drawings and models of Lilliputian  objects to explore the effect of rescaling on linear, area, and volume measures. They also contrast how things are measured with inches and feet, centimeters and meters, and the Lilliputian units described in Gulliver's journal. At the end of the phase, students demonstrate their growing knowledge of scale, measurement systems, and rescaling by writing a new story set in Lilliput.

Lands of the Large and Lands of the Little

Students examine photos from many different lands to figure out the scale factor that relates sizes in each land to sizes in Ourland. They explore scale factors that enlarge and scale factors that reduce sizes, using both integer and noninteger scales. They create displays showing size relationships among the various lands and systematize their understanding of the effect of rescaling on area and volume. Students end the unit by creating and presenting a display with 3-D objects from *Gulliver's Worlds.*

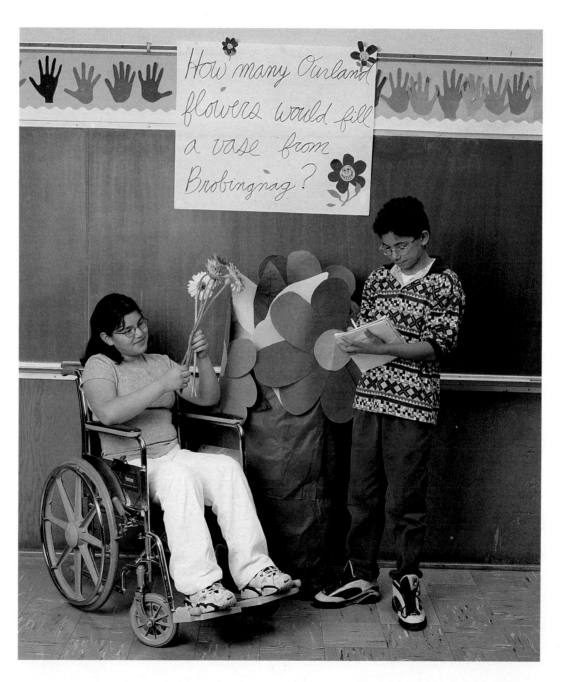

How many Ourland flowers would fill a vase from Brobingnag?

MathScape: *n:* A view of the world from a mathematical perspective.

Math Themes

Throughout Gulliver's Worlds, students work with the concepts of **Scale**, **Ratio**, and **Proportion** as they develop their understandings of proportional reasoning.

This unit focuses on situations in which the sizes of objects have **Proportional Relationships**. For example, each object in a land of giants might be 12 times as large as the comparable object in Ourland. To discover and apply these relationships, students employ their abilities to find, describe, and extend **Patterns**.

While measuring objects, rescaling their sizes, and making comparisons, students also explore the concept of **Dimension**. They measure and compare lengths, areas, and volumes, exploring the effect of rescaling on 1, 2, and 3 dimensional measures. The theme of **Multiple Representations** also comes into play as students represent size relationships and dimensions with numbers, ratios, words, drawings, and physical models.

Combining **Scale** and **Dimensions** leads to some mathematical surprises. For example, if the one-dimensional measures in Lilliput are one-tenth those in Ourland, how do the three-dimensional measures compare? How many Lilliputian loaves of bread are needed to supply as much bread as in one loaf from Ourland? The answer, as we will see in the unit, is far larger than most people would expect.

THE MATHSCAPE

Math Processes

Throughout the unit, students apply the processes of problem solving, visual thinking, and communication.

Some problems involve extracting information from stories or pictures to find size relationships. For example, what clues in the story can help us determine the relationship between the sizes of things in Ourland and in Brobdingnag? Several problems also involve strategies for estimating sizes. For example, what in Ourland is about as tall as the forty-foot-tall girl who takes care of Gulliver in Brobdingnag? Others involve strategies for rescaling. For example, how can we accurately rescale the size of an irregularly shaped object?

Throughout the unit, students describe and share their strategies for solving problems such as these. In addition, students are asked to write a letter to the King and Queen of Lilliput describing how we measure things in Ourland. Students also use their mathematical language to create their own stories describing imaginary adventures in some of the lands that incorporate accurate size information. Throughout the writing and problem solving activities, visual thinking is encouraged. For example, can you envision what it would look like inside a Brobdingnag classroom? How would your size compare to a pencil or a book in this land of giants?

Math Strands

Students' work in this unit involves three of the major mathematical content strands: Numbers and Operations, Geometry, Measurement, and Algebra.

As they visit each land, students collect information from stories and pictures about the sizes of things. They analyze this information in order to to determine proportional relationships among the sizes of things in different lands. In doing so, students work with simple direct variation functions, in which one variable is equal to so many times another.

Students use computation to predict the sizes of things in the different lands, to find the sizes in each dimension for their drawings and models, to determine whether statements about objects in a given land could be true, and to solve other types of problems. Many of these computations involve fractions. Students rescale objects using fractions to measure them accurately and working with noninteger proportional relationships, such as 4.5 to 1.

The activities of measuring lengths, areas, and volumes, comparing 1, 2, and 3 dimensional measures, and creating scale models (which are similar to the original objects, in the geometric sense of having the proportions) use key concepts from the geometry and measurement strands.

NCTM CURRICULUM STANDARDS FOR GRADES 5–8

The standards that correlate to the content in this unit are checked.

✔ Number and Operations

   Algebra

✔ Geometry

✔ Measurement

   Data Analysis and Probability

✔ Problem Solving

✔ Reasoning and Proof

✔ Communication

✔ Connections

✔ Representation

PREREQUISITES

It is helpful if students enter this unit with some experience in the following skills:

- Measurement of lengths using units from U.S. customary and metric systems

- Measurement of lengths using fractions of units from U.S. customary and metric systems

- Conversion of units within a measurement system

If your students need preliminary work with these skills, you may want to review:

hot words

- length
- measurement units

hot topics

- Length and Distance
- Geometry Tools

Have students review the unit overview on pages 276–277 in the Student Guide.

The following question is posed on page 276 of Gulliver's Worlds Student Guide: How big are things in Gulliver's Worlds? This question is investigated in the following pre-assessment activity, which generates class discussion and individual writing that helps reveal how much students know about measurement, scale, proportion, and area relationships.

Materials

Per student:

- A Letter from Gulliver, Reproducible R9
- scissors
- ruler
- drawing paper (11″ × 17″)

Prerequisite Check

Distribute Reproducible R9, A Letter from Gulliver and have students work in groups to describe the measurements of each of the stamps and the Ourland envelope. Encourage each group to use both the U.S. customary and metric system to describe at least one stamp.

If you notice students confusing the terms length and width or having trouble converting units within a system, you might need to review aspects of measurement before beginning the unit. Students do not need to be able to convert between measurement systems to be successful in this unit.

Performance Task

The following activity can be done individually or in pairs. Explain to students that they will be learning about and using scale in this unit, and that this is an example of the kind of problems they will be solving in the unit. Students should be able to complete this activity at various levels: manipulatives, diagrams, and algorithms. Have students use their materials to complete the following tasks:

- Come up with a way to figure out how big an envelope would be in Colossal City.
- Describe in writing and pictures how you figured out the size of the envelope.

You may need to point out that stamps and envelopes in the various lands only come in one standard size. You should also keep extra copies of the reproducible and paper on hand, as some students will immediately begin to cut up their materials.

In the Assessment pages that accompany this unit, see Pre-assessment page A4 for assessment information and sample student work.

PLANNING AND PACING

ALTERNATIVE ROUTES THROUGH THE UNIT

Typically this unit takes approximately 20 class periods, each lasting 45 minutes.

Lesson	Pacing (days)	Reproducibles	Materials (per student)	Materials (per group or class)
Pre-Assessment	1	R9, R8*	scissors, ruler, 11" × 17" drawing paper	
Lesson 1	1	R11, R9*	ruler	yardstick or tape measure*
Lesson 2	2	R12	pencils, markers, or crayons, ruler, large sheet of paper	
Lesson 3	1	R13		yardstick, tape measure, or string
Lesson 4	2	R14, R20, R2*, R5*		yardstick, tape measure, or string
Lesson 5	1	R15, R16	ruler	yardstick or tape measure*
Lesson 6	1	R17		rulers (metric and customary)
Lesson 7	1	R18	ruler, sheet of paper, scissors	
Lesson 8	1	R19, R21, R3*, R6*		yardstick, tape measure, or string
Lesson 9	2			pencils, markers, or crayons, ruler, scissors, glue or tape, large sheet of paper
Lesson 10	2		ruler, large sheet of paper	pencils, markers, or crayons, paper (snapshot size), ruler
Lesson 11	2			graph paper, 50–100 Rainbow Centimeter Cubes*
Lesson 12	2	R22, R23, R4*, R6*	ruler or tape measure	art materials*
Post-Assessment	1			

Unit Resource Manager

*Optional items: R2—Skill Quiz 1, R3—Skill Quiz 2, R4—Skill Quiz 3, R5—Student Assessment Criteria 1, R6—Student Assessment Criteria 2 and 3, R8—Family Letter

---

I wanted my class to just focus on scale and proportion in this unit. I found that by cutting the three lessons that dealt with area and volume and excluding certain steps that explored area and volume relationships (i.e., Lesson 2, Step 5; Lesson 3, Step 5), I was able to significantly shorten the time needed to complete the unit.

Phase One: Shorten Lessons 2 and 3.
Phase Two: Cut Lessons 6 and 7.
Phase Three: Cut Lesson 11.
Time: 16 class sessions □

I only had time for two phases, so I decided to focus only on enlarging scales and then go right to the final project. I also challenged some students to explore the world of Lilliput as an extension and create a final project that used a reducing scale.

Phase One: Remains as is.
Phase Two: Cut this Phase.
Phase Three: Cut Lesson 10.
Time: 14 class sessions □

0100101010100101010001010110111010100111101010101010101010101011110101010101010101011110101010101010101010101111

Lesson 5 Finding Ratios

Spreadsheet

A spreadsheet like the one at the top right can be used in Lesson 5 to discover the ratio of objects on Lilliput to objects in Ourland. Enter the name of the items in column A, the size of the items in Lilliput in column B, and the size of corresponding items in Ourland in column C. In column E, enter the formula =B2/C2 to compute the ratio. Use the drag fill feature to copy the formula through cell E7. The spreadsheet calculates that the ratio is approximately 0.083.

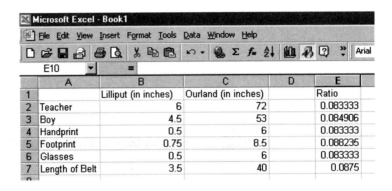

	A	B	C	D	E
1		Lilliput (in inches)	Ourland (in inches)		Ratio
2	Teacher	6	72		0.083333
3	Boy	4.5	53		0.084906
4	Handprint	0.5	6		0.083333
5	Footprint	0.75	8.5		0.088235
6	Glasses	0.5	6		0.083333
7	Length of Belt	3.5	40		0.0875

Next, the students can use a spreadsheet like the one at the bottom right to calculate what the measure of objects from Ourland would be in Lilliput. Enter the name of the item in column A and the measurement from Ourland in column B. In column C, calculate the measure of the object in Lilliput by entering the formula =0.083*B2. Use the drag fill feature to copy this formula to cell C7.

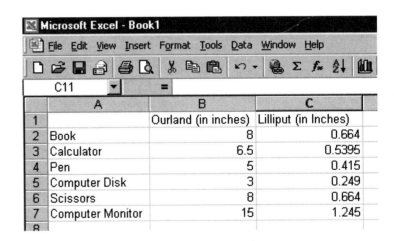

	A	B	C
1		Ourland (in inches)	Lilliput (in Inches)
2	Book	8	0.664
3	Calculator	6.5	0.5395
4	Pen	5	0.415
5	Computer Disk	3	0.249
6	Scissors	8	0.664
7	Computer Monitor	15	1.245

Calculator

Lesson 7 Area of Circles

Students can use an application called *Geoboard* for the TI-73 calculator to investigate how the area of a circle changes when the radius changes. Students do not need to know the formula for area in order to explore the scale relationships in this geometry activity.

To use the program, press the $\boxed{\text{APPS}}$ key and use the down-arrow key to highlight *GEOBOARD*. Then press $\boxed{\text{ENTER}}$ and start the application by pressing any key. Press the right arrow key to highlight *CIR*. Use the down-arrow key to select the desired radius. (It's best to start with 1). Use the down-arrow key again to choose the number of "pegs". The higher the number of pegs, the more accurate your measurement will be. For this particular activity, 6 pegs should be sufficient.   Press $\boxed{\text{GRAPH}}$. Your screen will look like this.

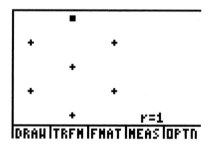

The keys in the $\boxed{\text{Y=}}$ row of the calculator correspond to the menu on the screen. Press $\boxed{\text{Y=}}$ [Draw] to open the Draw function. Then connect all of the exterior pegs by toggling the $\boxed{\text{Y=}}$ and the right arrow key repeatedly until the blinking cursor is back at the top and you have constructed a polygon that approximates a circle. End the

Draw function by pressing the $\boxed{\text{GRAPH}}$ key. To find the area, press $\boxed{\text{TRACE}}$ to select the Measurement functions. Use the down arrow to highlight 2:*Area.* Press $\boxed{\text{ENTER}}$ twice to view the formulated area. (Note: The area is not 3.14 because the polygon is an approximated circle.)

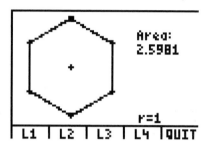

Have students record the radius and the area in a table, repeating this process using different radii lengths.

After students complete the activity, you may want to ask discussion questions like the following.

- If the radius is twice as long, will the area be twice as great? (no)

- What does this result tell us about the scale factor? (If the radius is doubled, the area increases by a scale factor of 4.)

MathScape Online

For a link to the TI Web site, and additional technology activities, visit:
www.mathscape1.com/technology

August 29, 1702

We finally sighted land again today. We went ashore near a small creek. I was gone only a short time. Yet when I headed back toward the landing site, the sailors were already rowing frantically out to sea. I could see a huge creature chasing them through the water. It stopped, though, at a sharp reef, and so the sailors escaped.

This was, I admit, of small comfort to me, because I was now alone. Fearing for my safety, I scampered inland. Beyond a steep hill, I discovered tall stalks, about eighteen feet high. They appeared to be wheat. I reached a stone stairway, but finding each step to rise six feet, I was unable to climb it. The trees along its edge were so tall I could not guess their height.

Lemuel Gulliver

MATH BACKGROUND

Scale Factors

As students collect data from Gulliver's journal about the sizes of things in Brobdingnag and compare their data to the sizes of things in Ourland (Lesson 1), they begin exploring a central mathematical concept of this unit, the scale factor. A scale factor (sometimes just called a *scale*) tells you how big something is in relationship to something else. More technically, the scale factor is the ratio that describes the relationship between sizes, such as 8 to 1 or 5 to 2 (often written as 8:1 or 5:2).

Rescaling

Students can measure the sizes of objects in Ourland, but in order to create a life-size Brobdingnag object (Lesson 2), they need to rescale, or use the scale factor to adjust the size of the original object.

One strategy for rescaling can be called *mark and measure*. To find the size of a Brobdingnag object, students use the object from Ourland and mark off each dimension by 10 or 12 (depending on the scale factor they are using). This works well with rectangular objects, but can be difficult with irregularly shaped objects.

Another strategy for rescaling can be called *measure and multiply*. Students using this approach measure each dimension of the Ourland object and then multiply each measure by the scale factor. With this approach, students will find they need to take careful measurements. A small error in the original measurement, when multiplied by the scale factor, can result in a large error in the final product.

The effects of rescaling can be surprising. The rescaled object often looks larger than students may have expected. For example, in the illustration below, the Titianian man is drawn at a scale of 4:1 to the Ourland man. However, since both the width and the height are rescaled by 4, the area of the larger man is 16 times that of the smaller one. (Area and volume are explored further in Phases Two and Three of this unit.)

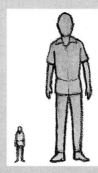

Ourland man: 6 feet
Titianian man: 24 feet

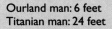 Please note that for this phase, all answers provided are based on a scale factor of 1:12. If any of your students decides to use another scale factor, such as 1:10, answers will not match the answers provided here but may still be correct with regard to the scale factor being used.

Imagine a world in which everything is so large that you would be as small as a mouse. How can you predict how large things will be in this land?

In this phase you will learn to figure out a scale factor that describes how sizes of things are related. You will use the scale factor to create life-size drawings, solve problems, and write stories.

Brobdingnag

WHAT'S THE MATH?

Investigations in this section focus on:

DATA COLLECTION

- Gathering information from a story
- Organizing data to find patterns

MEASUREMENT and ESTIMATION

- Measuring with inches, feet, and fractions of inches
- Estimating the sizes of large objects

SCALE and PROPORTION

- Finding the scale factor that describes the relationship between sizes
- Applying the scale factor to predict sizes of objects
- Creating scale drawings
- Exploring the effect of rescaling on area and volume

MathScape Online
mathscape1.com/self_check_quiz

AT A GLANCE

LESSON 1

The Sizes of Things in Brobdingnag

Students read the first parts of Gulliver's journal and use clues from the journal to determine a scale factor that relates the sizes of things in Brobdingnag to the sizes of things in Ourland. They use this scale factor to estimate the sizes of other things in Brobdingnag and to make comparisons between Ourland and Brobdingnag.

Mathematical Goals

- Identify and interpret mathematical information in a story.
- Organize data to identify patterns.
- Measure using inches, feet, and fractions of inches.
- Estimate sizes.
- Learn the concept of a scale factor.

MATERIALS

PER STUDENT

- ruler
- Reproducible R11
- Reproducible R9 (optional)

PER GROUP

- yardstick (optional)
- tape measure (optional)

LESSON 2

A Life-Size Object in Brobdingnag

Students continue to learn about Gulliver's life in Brobdingnag. Using careful measurements and the scale factor, they make actual-size drawings of objects from Brobdingnag. Students describe in writing how they made their objects the right sizes, and consider how many Ourland objects they would need to cover the Brobdingnag version.

Mathematical Goals

- Measure lengths accurately to fractions of an inch.
- Create scale drawings.
- Investigate the effect of rescaling on area.

MATERIALS

PER STUDENT

- pencils, markers, or crayons
- ruler
- large sheet of paper
- Reproducible R12

PREPARATION

Gather several objects for students to rescale in a 2-D drawing. Rectangular flat objects are easiest to rescale: computer disks, cards, calculators, cassettes. Round flat objects can be given as a challenge: coins, watch face, ring, or bracelet.

LESSON 3

How Big Is "Little" Glumdalclitch?

Students meet Glumdalclitch, Gulliver's 9-year-old friend who stands just under 40 feet tall, and set out using estimation techniques to find a building, tree, or pole that is about her height. They also explore area and volume relationships, considering, for example, how many of our shoe boxes would fit inside one of Glumdalclitch's.

Mathematical Goals

- Estimate the sizes of large objects.
- Communicate estimation strategies.
- Compare uses of estimation and measurement.
- Explore length, area, and volume relationships.

MATERIALS

PER STUDENT

- Reproducible R13

PER GROUP

- yardsticks, tape measures, or string

PREPARATION

Students will need to go outside for this activity. You may want to reserve the gym or multiuse room for this activity, or assign this part of the activity for homework.

LESSON 4

Telling Tales in Brobdingnag

Students continue their exploration of scale by determining whether headlines about Gulliver's experiences in Brobdingnag could be true or are unbelievable. Students write their own stories about a visit to Brobdingnag, using measurement, estimation, and scale to ensure their mathematical accuracy. For assessment purposes, students report the dimensions of the objects in their stories and describe the strategies they used to determine the sizes of Brobdingnag objects.

Mathematical Goals

- Measure and estimate lengths of objects.
- Rescale objects using a scale factor.
- Demonstrate understanding of area and volume.
- Incorporate accurate size information into stories.
- Communicate mathematical ideas in a story.

MATERIALS

PER STUDENT

- Reproducibles R5, R14, R20

PER GROUP

- yardstick, tape measure, or string

1 LESSON

Determining the Scale Factor

From Science class and museums, some students were familiar with scale models of things such as the solar system, molecules, the heart, and the eye. From Social Studies class, they had used scales on maps and globes. ☐

I showed a small section of the video, Honey, I Blew Up the Kid, to help students imagine a "Brobdingnagian" in Ourland. Some students remarked on how the kid in the movie grew larger in each scene, but were unable to articulate the concept of scale factor. ☐

I had students work in pairs, reading the story aloud and gathering measurement clues. This helped those students who do not read English well. The illustrations also helped these students understand the story. ☐

The Sizes of Things in Brobdingnag

Have students review the phase overview on pages 278–279 in the Student Guide.

1 Discussing Situations and Stories Using Scale

Explain that in this unit, Gulliver's journal entries are adapted from Jonathan Swift's famous novel, *Gulliver's Travels.* In Swift's book, originally written as a political satire, Gulliver travels to the lands of the giants and of the tiny people, and describes them in his journal. Have students list stories and movies in which the characters or sets are a different scale than normal. You may want to have them discuss other scale models they have seen. They are likely to be familiar with model trains, doll houses, globes, and other scale models.

Some examples of stories using scale include *The Borrowers; Honey, I Shrunk the Kids; Indian in the Cupboard; The BFG; Paul Bunyon;* and *Alice in Wonderland.* Such stories can be found in all parts of the world, and many have been made into movies.

2 Gathering Clues from Gulliver's Journal

Students should read both the phase introduction, Student Guide page 278, and the journal entry for this lesson to search for clues about the sizes of things in Brobdingnag. Help them to identify the clues with questions like the following:

- What clues can we find in the story about the sizes of things in Brobdingnag?

- Which objects in the story give you the best sense of the sizes of things in Brobdingnag? Are some objects easier to imagine than others?

homework options

LESSON HOMEWORK
Page 308

hot topics

- *Fractions and Equivalent Fractions (2•1)*
  Exercises 10–16
- *Comparing and Ordering Fractions (2•2)*
  Exercises 1–4, 8–10

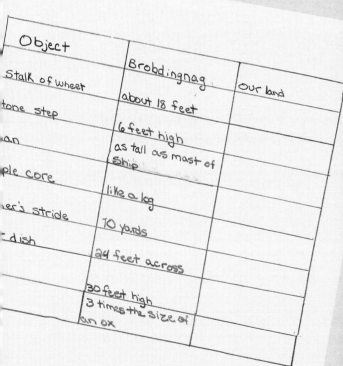

Object	Brobdingnag	Our land
Stalk of wheat	about 18 feet	
...tone step	6 feet high	
...an	as tall as mast of ship	
...ple core	like a log	
...er's stride	10 yards	
...dish	24 feet across	
	30 feet high 3 times the size of an ox	

1 The Sizes of Things in Brobdingnag

DETERMINING THE SCALE FACTOR

How well can you picture in your mind the events described in Gulliver's journal entry? Here you will gather clues from the journal entry about the sizes of things in Brobdingnag. As you compare sizes of things in Brobdingnag to sizes in Ourland, you will learn about scale.

August 29, 1702

I had not a moment to rest, as another monster was approaching. I now saw that in form he resembled a human being. It was his size—as tall as a ship's mast—that made him appear to be a monster. Scared and confused, I backed away, tripping over an apple core that lay like a log behind me. As I stood up again, the giant began cutting wheat with a great scythe. With every stride he traveled about ten yards closer to me, and I was faced with either being trampled on or cut in two. Therefore, I gave up my hiding place and shouted for his attention.

280

I used the overhead projector to demonstrate the idea of scale factor. I drew a 4" × 6" rectangle on a transparency, and had students measure the projected rectangle to give the scale factor between the actual drawn one and the projected one. We experimented with moving the overhead projector to different locations to see how the scale factor changed. □

We discussed which objects provided the best comparisons. For example, students felt that cats varied in size, and they did not really know how big an ox is, so that would not help them find the scale factor. They thought that stair steps and table heights did not vary much, so those would be good. They set out to measure steps and table heights to get accurate data. This led to Michael's rule: "An inch in Ourland becomes a foot in Brobdingnag." □

Isaac said the pencil would be about as tall as his father. Jennifer said that the pencil box would be about the size of the tent she used on her camping trip. Clearly, the students were getting a clear idea of what it would be like to visit Brobdingnag. □

student page

3 Comparing Sizes to Determine a Scale Factor

Have students create a chart and use the story to compare the sizes of objects in Brobdingnag to the sizes of objects in Ourland. Help them to use the information on their charts to determine a scale factor that relates the sizes of objects in the two lands. Discuss with students the example in the Student Guide of a model train in the scale of 20:1, and explain that we read this scale factor as "twenty to one."

Even if students work carefully and measure accurately, they will come up with scale factors ranging from 10:1 to 12:1. You may want to point out that sizes of things vary. For example, some tables are higher than others, some men take longer strides than others, and so on. Although students may be working with different scale factors, for clarity, the solutions in this guide use a scale factor of 12:1.

An Answer Key for items 1–3 can be found on Assessment page A21.

4 Finding the Sizes of Other Objects in Brobdingnag

Have students select four objects in the classroom and list the measurements in the Ourland column of their charts. Provide a yardstick or tape measure to help them measure the lengths, widths, and heights of the objects. Have students fill in the remainder of the chart using the scale factor from Step 3 to calculate both the scale-size and actual-size measurements of as many objects as they can.

You may want to teach students a quick to way to compute fractions using a ruler. For example, to multiply $\frac{3}{4}$ inch by 10, start at 0, count off $\frac{3}{4}$ inches 10 times, and where you end up on the ruler ($7\frac{1}{2}''$) is the answer.

5 Visualizing Brobdingnag Objects in Ourland

Ask students to think of objects in Ourland that are about the same size as each Brobdingnag object on their chart. Then ask them to visualize whether each Brobdingnag object would fit in the classroom, using questions such as the following:

- Would the giant-sized object fit on a student desk?

- Would the giant-sized object fit in the door?

- Would the giant-sized object fill the whole classroom?

- *determine accurate and complete measurements from the journal entry?*
- *measure with and convert between feet, inches, and fractions of inches?*
- *make realistic comparisons between sizes?*
- *use scale consistently with accurate computations?*

See *Gulliver's Worlds* Assessment page A5 for assessment information.

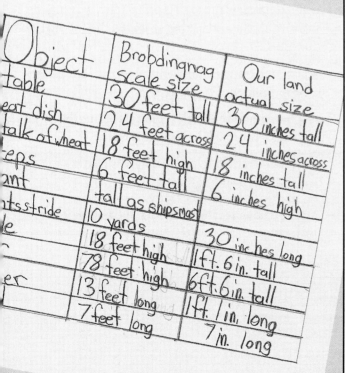

Compare Sizes to Determine a Scale Factor

A scale factor is a ratio that tells how the sizes of things are related. For example, some model trains use a 20:1 scale factor. This means that each part on the real train is 20 times as large as the same part on the model train. Follow these steps to find the scale factor that relates sizes in Brobdingnag to sizes in Ourland.

> How are sizes of things in Brobdingnag related to sizes in Ourland?

1 Make a chart with three columns. Column 1 is for the name of each object. Column 2 is for the size of the object in Brobdingnag. Column 3 is for the size of the corresponding object in Ourland.

2 Fill out column 1 and column 2 with clues you found in the story about the sizes of objects in Brobdingnag. Measure or estimate how big each of the objects would be in Ourland. Enter that information in column 3.

3 Use the information in your chart to figure out a scale factor that tells how sizes of things in Brobdingnag are related to sizes in Ourland.

Object	Brobdingnag	Ourland
Stalk of wheat	About 18 feet	

How big would an Ourland object be in Brobdingnag?

hot **words** | scale size
scale factor

H⬛**omework**
page 308

A Life-Size Object in Brobdingnag

Some students measured each side of the object, multiplied the measure by the scale factor, and then marked that side on the paper. Others used the object itself, marked a starting point on the paper, placed the object end to end 12 times, and marked the ending point. Others used string to measure the original objects and then cut a piece of string 12 times the size. □

Students were intrigued by the idea of using different scales for length and width. They realized that an object would come out distorted, "like it had been stretched out" or "like you look in one of those funny mirrors." □

1 Reviewing Size Estimation and Rescaling

As a class or individually read Gulliver's journal, and use the following questions to help students compare the sizes of objects in the story to objects found in the classroom. To review the concept of scale factor from Lesson 1, you may want to have students estimate how large other objects within the classroom might be in Brobdingnag and imagine how Gulliver might use them.

- What objects in the story are also in the classroom?

- Which Brobdingnag object could fit into the classroom?

- Which Brobdingnag objects would be too big for the classroom? Where would they fit?

2 Choosing and Rescaling an Object

Have each student choose a small object from a collection of objects you have gathered (see Phase One At a Glance, page 279A). Encourage each student to carefully measure the object and come up with a way to determine its size in Brobdingnag. You may want to begin the activity by choosing one object and asking students the following questions:

- How tall do you think this object would be in Brobdingnag? How wide?

- What object in the classroom is about the same size as this object in Brobdingnag?

- How could you figure out the exact size of this object in Brobdingnag?

As you prepare for this activity, keep in mind that small rectangular objects (i.e., computer disks, erasers, index cards, etc.) are easier to rescale than circular or irregular objects.

homework options

LESSON HOMEWORK
Page 309

hot topics
- *Size and Scale (8•6)*
  Exercises 1–3, 5, 6

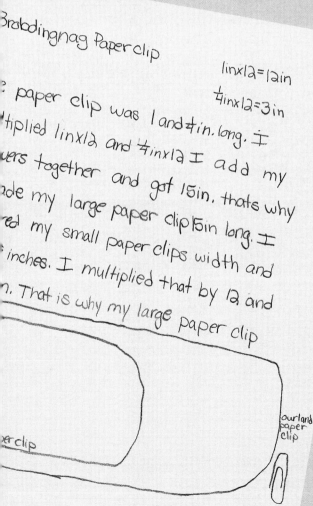

Brobdingnag Paperclip

$1 in \times 12 = 12 in$

$\frac{1}{4} in \times 12 = 3 in$

...? paper clip was 1 and $\frac{1}{4}$in. long. I

...tiplied 1in$\times$12 and $\frac{1}{4}$in$\times$12 I add my

...ers together and got 15in. thats why

...de my large paper clip 15in long. I

...red my small paper clips width and

... inches. I multiplied that by 12 and

... That is why my large paper clip

ourland paper clip

...erclip

2 A Life-Size Object in Brobdingnag

RESCALING THE SIZES OF OBJECTS

The story continues as Gulliver describes more events from his life in Brobdingnag. In the last lesson, you figured out how sizes in Brobdingnag relate to sizes in Ourland. In this lesson you will use what you know to create a life-size drawing of a Brobdingnag object.

August 30, 1702

I soon became like one more member of the giant's family. In an effort to gain some much-needed privacy, I leaned two large envelopes against a stack of books that measured 10 feet high. Crawling under the envelopes, I had a spacious shelter from prying eyes and a measure of peace. I then made a roomy bed of a small diary with an abandoned eraser as my pillow. Looking around my improvised room, I quickly did a calculation in my head and determined a piece of note paper would be the ideal covering for my long awaited nap. Unfortunately, at this great size the paper was like cardboard and left me longing for my wool blanket back home.

282

Students found that small errors in the original measurement could make their drawings look "weird." We discussed the need to measure to the nearest eighth or sixteenth of an inch. An error of just $\frac{1}{8}$ inch in the initial measurement would become an error of $1\frac{1}{2}$ inches in the large drawing. Students also noted that measuring precisely was harder when working with curved or irregularly shaped objects. □

Students quickly found that curved objects, such as a coin or a paper clip, are much trickier than rectangular objects, such as a small calculator or a computer disk. With rectangular objects, students used a measure-and-multiply approach. With curved objects, students tended to use the object itself. For example, one group made an arrangement of pennies in the shape of a plus sign and used that as a guide for drawing a circle. It wasn't exact, but it was a good approximation. □

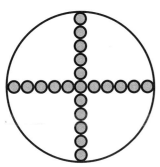

student page

3 Making a Life-Size Drawing

When drawing and labeling the measurements of a Brobdingnag object, most students should be able to find a way to check that their drawings and measurements are accurate. If students make mistakes measuring or calculating one part of the object, they should immediately see their mistakes in their drawings because they will appear out of proportion. Finally, have students describe in writing how they made their life-size drawings and checked to make sure their measurements were correct.

student page

4 Investigating the Effect of Rescaling on Area

Students will use their drawings to investigate area by determining how many of the original objects it takes to cover the Brobdingnag object completely. Encourage students to include diagrams or calculations with their description of how they investigated the area of the object.

> Students may be surprised that the number of Ourland objects required to cover the Brobdingnag object is many more than the scale factor. Students who rescaled a rectangular object may be able to find that the number is the square of the scale factor. At this point, students should begin contrasting changes in length with changes in area.

5 Discussing Rescaling Strategies

To help students write about the effect of rescaling on area, use the following questions for a small-group or class discussion. Students should focus on the need to measure precisely, since small errors in the original measurements will result in large errors in the Brobdingnag object.

- Were some objects more difficult to rescale than others?

- How did you rescale circular or irregular shapes?

- How did you check whether your scale drawing was accurate in size?

- If your measurement of the Ourland object was off by $\frac{1}{2}$ inch, what would happen to the drawing of the Brobdingnag object?

- What would happen if you used different scales for the width and for the length?

what to look for

DO STUDENTS' DRAWINGS AND REPORTS REFLECT:

- *an ability to accurately measure objects?*
- *an ability to rescale objects using a scale factor?*
- *a logical system to check rescaling?*
- *an emerging understanding of area?*

See *Gulliver's Worlds* Assessment page A5 for assessment information.

Brobingnang Penny Area

When I tried to find out how many pennies it would take to cover my giant penny, I ran out of pennies. I divided my drawing into fourths and covered one fourth with the outlines of my penny and multiplied that number by four.

32 × 4 = 148

Make a Life-Size Drawing

Choose an object from Ourland that is small enough to fit in your pocket or in your hand. What would be the size of your object in Brobdingnag? Make a life-size drawing of the Brobdingnag object.

How can you figure out the size of a Brobdingnag object?

1. Make the size of your drawing as accurate as possible. Label the measurements.

2. After you finish your drawing, figure out a way to check that your drawing and measurements are accurate.

3. Write a short description about how you determined the size of your drawing and how you checked that the drawing was accurate.

Investigate the Effect of Rescaling on Area

How many of the Ourland objects does it take to cover all of the Brobdingnag object? Use your drawing and the original Ourland object to investigate this question. Write about how you figured out how many Ourland objects it took to cover the Brodingnag object.

BROBDINGNAG Discovered A.D. 1703

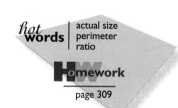

hot **words** | actual size
perimeter
ratio

H·**mework**

page 309

How Big Is "Little" Glumdalclitch?

3 LESSON

Estimating Lengths, Areas, and Volumes

One group found a clever way to measure the height of the flagpole in the school yard. They saw that a rope goes all the way up to the flag at the top of the pole—the rope that's used to raise and lower the flag. The measured the amount of rope they pull in one pull and then counted the number of pulls needed to get the flag all the way down. They checked by raising the flag back up. □

Some of my students came up with sophisticated estimation strategies:

"I measured the bottom six feet of the flagpole, and then I estimated that six feet was about $\frac{1}{7}$ of the total height of the flagpole. I wrote 6 feet × 7 and got 42 feet as my estimate." □

1 Visualizing Brobdingnag Objects in Ourland

After students have read Gulliver's journal, you may want to use the following questions to help them visualize Glumdalclitch's height.

- What objects in Ourland are about the same size as Glumdalclitch?

- Does that seem right for a 9-year-old girl?

- What other clues in the story help give you a sense of Glumdalclitch's size?

2 Developing Strategies to Estimate Size

To help students find a tall object in Ourland that is close to Glumdalclitch's height (40 feet), have them estimate the height of three tall objects (such as a telephone pole, a tree, a building) and determine which object comes closest to Glumdalclitch's size. Have them write a brief description of the strategy they used to estimate the height of the Ourlandian objects.

Estimating tall objects works best as an outdoor or homework activity. For an indoor alternative, students might estimate the heights of stairwells or the ceiling in the gymnasium or auditorium.

3 Discussing Estimation and Measurement Strategies

You can use the following questions for a class discussion, or have students interview each other. Help students to think about the differences between estimation and measurement.

- What strategy did you use to make your estimates?

- How is estimation different from measurement? Why might you decide to estimate something rather than measure it? Why might you decide to measure rather than estimate?

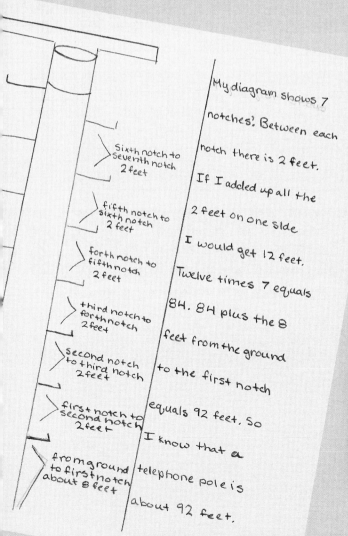

My diagram shows 7 notches. Between each notch there is 2 feet.

If I added up all the 2 feet on one side I would get 12 feet.

Twelve times 7 equals 84. 84 plus the 8 feet from the ground to the first notch equals 92 feet. So I know that a telephone pole is about 92 feet.

Sixth notch to seventh notch 2 feet

fifth notch to sixth notch 2 feet

forth notch to fifth notch 2 feet

third notch to forth notch 2 feet

second notch to third notch 2 feet

first notch to second notch 2 feet

from ground to first notch about 8 feet

3 How Big Is "Little" Glumdalclitch?

ESTIMATING LENGTHS, AREAS, AND VOLUMES

What if Glumdalclitch visited Ourland? Would she fit in your classroom? Drawing a picture of "little" Glumdalclitch in actual Ourland measurements would take a great deal of paper. To get a sense of the size of a very large object, it is sometimes easier to use estimation.

November 25, 1702

My first impression of the girl in the family proved to be correct. She was very good-natured, kind in spirit, and patient in teaching me her language. She was considered small for her age, being just under forty feet tall. Therefore I called her Glumdalclitch, which I learned means "Little Nurse" in her language. She called me Grildrig, meaning "Little Puppet."

284

Most of my students were familiar with area and volume, but few had investigated the relationships between the different measurements. I had my students use their scale drawings from Lesson 2 to explain the differences between scale factor, area, volume, and the corresponding measurements to a partner. ☐

student page

4 Using Estimation to Solve Problems

Have students use estimation to solve each of the problems listed. They should describe in writing how they found each answer. Encourage them to include diagrams, a clear explanation of each problem, and their measurements or estimation strategy.

As students explore these questions, they develop an intuitive sense of how a scale factor affects the actual size of things. They should discover that a large number (far more than the scale factor of 10 or 12) of Ourland-size objects is required to cover or fill the corresponding Brobdingnag object. For example, Glumdalclitch's mattress must be at least 40 feet long; its width, which would also reflect Brobdingnag's larger scale, must be at least 20 feet. Whether or not the floor of the classroom is large enough to accommodate a mattress of this size, students will recognize that familiar Ourland-size mattresses must be placed side to side as well as end to end to fill the same space. This suggests a product of two factors. Similarly, to fill a Brobdingnag shoe box, Ourland-size shoe boxes would have to be packed in columns, rows, and layers to fill the scaled-up width, length, and height of the larger box. This suggests taking the product of three scale factors.

5 Contrasting Lengths, Areas, and Volumes

Have students reflect on why so many Ourland objects are needed to cover, and even more to fill, a Brobdingnag object. If you feel your students are ready, you can use this investigation to introduce the terminology and point out the contrasts among linear measurement (one dimension), area measurement (two dimensions: length and

width) and volume measurement (three dimensions: length, width, and height). Students will reexamine linear, area, and volume relationships in Lesson 7, and the following concepts can also be introduced at that point.

As students explain their reasoning, you may want to clarify the following concepts, using cubes or diagrams.

A scale factor refers to a change in one dimension, length. If the scale factor is 4, we can put 4 of the small objects end to end to match the length of the large object.

Scale Factor

When we want to know how many small objects it would take to cover a large object, we need to consider two dimensions, length and width. If the scale factor is 4, we would need 4 rows with 4 in each row to cover the large object with small objects. When we consider these two dimensions, we are comparing areas.

Area

When we want to know how many small objects it would take to fill a large object, we need to consider three dimensions: length, width, and height. If a scale factor is 4, we would need 4 layers. Each layer would have 4 rows, and each row would have 4 objects. When we consider these three dimensions, we are comparing volumes.

Volume

what to look for

DO STUDENTS' SOLUTIONS REFLECT:

- *an ability to estimate the size of a very large object?*
- *clear communication of an estimation strategy?*
- *an accurate relationship between original size and rescaled size?*
- *an understanding of the differences among length, area, and volume?*

See *Gulliver's Worlds* Assessment page A5 for assessment information.

Glumdalclitch Mattress

Mattress

I think a mattress for Glu... would NOT fit in the ... my mattress ...

It would (144) ourland mattresses to cover a Brob mattress

Brobdingnag Mattress

Use Estimation to Solve Problems

Estimate the size of each Brobdingnag object. Answer the questions about how the size of the Brobdingnag object compares to size of the same Ourland object and explain how you found each answer.

1 Could a mattress that would fit Glumdalclitch fit in the classroom? How much of the floor would it cover? How many Ourland mattresses would it take to cover the same amount of floor?

2 How big would Glumdalclitch's notebook be? How many sheets of our notebook paper would we need to tape together to make one sheet for her notebook?

3 How big a shoe box do you think Glumdalclitch might have? How many of our shoe boxes would fit inside hers?

4 How many slices of our bread would it take to make one slice of bread big enough for Glumdalclitch to eat?

Why are so many Ourland objects needed to cover or to fill a Brobdingnag object?

> **How do objects from Ourland and Brobdingnag compare in length, area, and volume?**

BROBDINGNAG Discovered AD 1703

hot **words** | area

H○mework

page 310

4

LESSON

Using Accurate Sizes in Creative Stories

I wrote a few headlines on the board to help students see the connection between unbelievable stories and the Brobdingnag headlines. In each case I asked students to figure out the largest and smallest the Ourland object could be. We used that information to set the possible range of sizes in Brobdingnag. If the headline had a size out of that range, it was labeled unbelievable. ☐

Some of the headlines involved classroom objects that students were able to measure directly and then rescale. However, other problems referred to things that are not available in the classroom. I had my students either estimate the size or look up the information in an almanac. ☐

Telling Tales in Brobdingnag

1 Identifying Correct Math Information in Stories

Discuss the idea of unbelievable stories, or "Tall Tales"—in this case, headlines describing Gulliver's travels that may be exaggerated. Have students read the final entry for Brobdingnag in Gulliver's journal, and have them brainstorm about the kinds of challenges Gulliver faced during his stay in Brobdingnag because of his size. Use the following questions to explore what stories could be added to the journal that would be believable.

- What animal in Ourland would be about the same size as a Brobdingnag wasp?

- How big would a Brobdingnag spider be?

- Could a Brobdingnag spider be as big as a car in Ourland? Why or why not?

You may need to make it clear that when you are talking about believable scenes, you mean from a mathematically consistent point of view based on the scale factor established in the journal so far. An exaggerated headline would involve a scale relationship that was inconsistent with the one established.

2 Examining a Statement for Accuracy

Distribute Reproducible R20, Headlines, and have students determine whether each statement about Gulliver in Brobdingnag is believable or unbelievable. As they research and explore the claims in each headline, they gain a better understanding of the scale factor in Brobdingnag. To save time, you may assign this step as homework.

An Answer Key for Reproducible R20 can be found on Assessment page A21.

Headlines

a. Man Swims with Whale-Sized Goldfish

b. Traveler Reads Book that's as Tall as a two-story building

Shipwrecked Surgeon Dodges fork the Size of Shovel

Five-foot mouse Scares Visitor

Man Rides on Butterfly's back

Man floats on Raft Made of 12 pencils

4 Telling Tales in Brobdingnag

USING ACCURATE
SIZES IN CREATIVE
STORIES

Imagine how it would be for you to visit Brobdingnag.
By now you have a good understanding of the scale factor in Brobdingnag. You can use what you know to write your own story. You will see that good mathematical thinking is important in writing a believable story.

June 12, 1704

My size led to some frightening situations. One morning, I was sitting by the window when twenty giant wasps came flying into the room. Some of them carried off the sweet cake I was about to eat for breakfast. Others flew around my head, confusing me with the noise and threatening me with their stings. I killed four of them with my sword and drove the rest off. In other situations, my small size proved very useful. For example, I was once lowered in a bucket down the well to retrieve a ring that the princess had dropped accidentally. She was so happy when they pulled me back up and she saw her prized ring, which I had placed over my head and around my neck for safekeeping.

286

Most of my students used measurements in their scene and gave accurate estimates of Brobdingnag sizes.

"I was walking toward the front of the Brobdingnag classroom, hoping that the teacher would notice me. A giant log was in my way. I suddenly realized that the log was really a pencil that one of the young Brobdingnagians had dropped, for in a matter of seconds, a five foot long hand reached down to the floor. It began scrambling around, trying to find the pencil. Suddenly, the hand seized me by my knees! "I'll use this stubby pencil," the Brobdingnagian murmured, as it brought me up to the desk. I wanted to scream, but I couldn't get hold of my voice.

Without even looking at me, he (now I knew it was a he) absent-mindedly started to doodle on a piece of paper, using my feet as a tip. As the teacher walked by, he rapidly turned me around, and used my head as the eraser. "Ouch!" I yelled. Shocked, he dropped me. "I can't believe I actually survived the 28 foot drop from the desk to the floor!"

This student shows an ability to measure and an understanding of the concept of scale. □

3 Writing a Story Using Accurate Dimensions

As students brainstorm their stories, encourage them to write themselves into their adventure in Brobdingnag. Remind them to use accurate dimensions for the objects and include a believable title. To prepare students to write their stories, you may want to have a class discussion:

- How big would you be in comparison to Brobdingnagians your age?

- What size would a Brobdingnag chair be? a desk? a pencil?

- How large would handwriting be? Could you read it?

- If a giant pen dropped to the floor, what kind of sound would it make?

Have students keep a record of their measurements and calculations for their summaries at the end of the lesson.

4 Summarizing the Math Used in the Story

At the end of the story, have students summarize how they used measurement, estimation, and calculations to find the sizes of the objects in their stories. Encourage them to think of their writing as a demonstration of what they have learned in this phase about scale, proportion, and measurement.

Write a Story Using Accurate Dimensions

Choose one place in Brobdingnag. Imagine what it would be like to visit that place. Describe in detail the place and at least one adventure that happened to you there.

1 Write a story about Brobdingnag. Make the story believable by using accurate measurements for the objects you describe.

2 Include a size description of at least three objects found in that place.

3 Write a believable title. The title should include at least one size comparison between Brobdingnag and Ourland.

4 Record and check all of your measurements.

Summarize the Math Used in the Story

After you write your story, summarize how you used math to figure out the sizes of things in the story. Include the following in your summary:

- Make a table, list, or drawing showing the sizes of the three objects in both Ourland and Brobdingnag.

- Explain how you used scale, estimation, and measurement to figure out the sizes of these objects.

> **How can you use rescaling to write a story about Brobdingnag?**

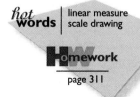

hot **words** | linear measure, scale drawing

Homework
page 311

PHASE TWO

August 5, 1706

Having been condemned by nature and fortune to a restless life, I took a post on the Antelope, a trading ship.

I had been spending much time on deck, until a storm suddenly came upon us. The ship sank on a reef, and I became separated from my crew. Pushed toward shore by the tide, I fell exhausted upon the softest and shortest grass I had ever seen. But before I could examine it further, I fell into a deep sleep.

When I awoke, I found my arms and legs strongly fastened to the ground. Even my hair was tied down. My frustration gave way to surprise as I saw who had done this. Hundreds of them were scattered on the ground around me. They looked like men in every way but one— they were a mere six inches tall.

Lemuel Gulliver

MATH BACKGROUND

Scale Factors that Reduce Sizes

This phase introduces Lilliput, a land in which things are smaller than in Ourland (Lesson 5). This leads students to working with a scale factor of approximately 1:10 or 1:12. For the sake of clarity, the answers provided for this phase are based on a scale factor of 1:12. If another scale factor is used, answers will vary accordingly. The convention that the Ourland size always comes last when writing a scale factor will help students communicate about scale factors without confusion. Working with a scale factor that reduces sizes this much requires students to measure carefully, using fractions of measurement units.

The Effects of Rescaling on Area and Volume

In Lesson 7, students are asked questions such as, "How many Lilliputian pieces of paper would be needed to make one sheet of writing paper for Gulliver?" and, "How many Lilliputian loaves of bread would be needed to equal the amount of bread in one Ourland loaf?" These questions lead students to explore the effects of rescaling on area and volume. This topic will be explored more systematically in Lesson 11 of the next phase.

Consider what happens when we rescale by a factor of 4.

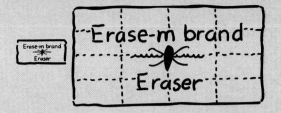

Erase-m brand
Eraser

Original eraser (left) rescaled by a factor of 4 (right)

It will take 4 rows of the original object, with 4 of the objects across each row, to cover the enlarged object completely. When we rescale by 4, we multiply both the width and the length by 4. Since $4 \times 4 = 16$, it would take 16 of the original size objects to cover the enlarged object completely. The area is increased by a factor of 16.

This pattern holds for any scale factor: area changes by the square of the scale factor. Therefore, if the scale factor is 2, the area is increased by a factor of 4; if the scale factor is 4, the area is increased by a factor of 16; if the scale factor is 10, the area is increased by a factor of 100.

Volume adds a third dimension, so that when an object is rescaled the volume changes by the cube of the scale factor. See the Math Background for Phase Three, page 299, for more information about volume.

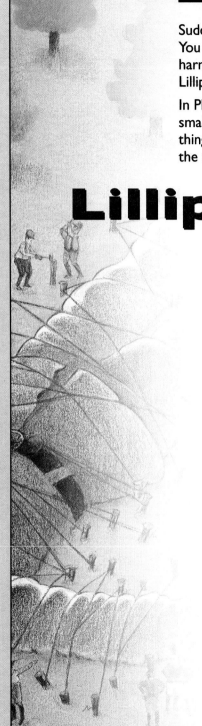

Suddenly you are in a world in which everything is tiny. You have to be careful where you step, so that you don't harm people or destroy houses. The name of this land is Lilliput.

In Phase Two, you will use a scale factor that makes things smaller. You will compare the different ways of measuring things using inches and feet, centimeters and meters and the measurement units used in Lilliput.

Lilliput

WHAT'S THE MATH?

Investigations in this section focus on:

DATA COLLECTION

- Gathering information from a story and pictures
- Organizing data to find patterns

MEASUREMENT and ESTIMATION

- Measuring accurately using fractions
- Comparing the U.S. customary and metric systems of measurement
- Estimating the sizes of objects
- Exploring area and volume measurements

SCALE and PROPORTION

- Working with a scale factor that reduces the sizes of objects
- Applying the scale factor to predict sizes of objects and to create a three-dimensional scale model
- Exploring the effect of rescaling on area and volume

MathScape Online
mathscape1.com/self_check_quiz

AT A GLANCE

LESSON 5

Sizing Up the Lilliputians

Students follow the adventures of Gulliver as he lands in Lilliput. They use written and pictorial clues in the story to determine the sizes of things in Lilliput, compare them to the sizes of things in Ourland, and determine the scale factor relating the sizes. Also, students combine their understandings of averages and scale to determine whether a Lilliputian child is of average height.

Mathematical Goals

- Identify and interpret mathematical information in stories.
- Apply measurement and estimation techniques.
- Apply concept of average (any or all of mean, median, or mode).
- Explore scale factors that reduce sizes—factors less than 1.

MATERIALS

PER STUDENT

- ruler
- Reproducibles R15–R16

PER GROUP

- yardstick (optional)
- tape measure (optional)

LESSON 6

Glum-gluffs and Mum-gluffs

Students read about meeting with the king and queen of Lilliput, who want to know how big things are in Ourland and how we measure them. Students draw a life-size Lilliputian object and then find an Ourland object of comparable size. They are then asked to explain our U.S. customary system of measurement and the metric system using words and drawings, and contrast them with the Lilliputian measurement units.

Mathematical Goals

- Accurately measure objects in standard and nonstandard units.
- Rescale objects.
- Describe and contrast the U.S. customary and metric systems of measurement.

MATERIALS

PER GROUP

- rulers (metric and customary)
- Reproducible R17

LESSON 7

Housing and Feeding Gulliver

Students compare linear, area, and volume measurements as they investigate what would be involved for the Lilliputians to feed and house Gulliver. Students create actual-size models to check answers to various problems involving 1-D, 2-D, and 3-D measurements.

Mathematical Goals

- Apply measurement and scaling.
- Create a 3-D scale model.
- Explore area and volume.

MATERIALS

PER STUDENT

- ruler
- sheet of paper
- scissors
- Reproducible R18

PREPARATION

You can extend this activity to incorporate various 3-D art media: papier mâché, clay, foil sculpture, and different modeling materials.

LESSON 8

Seeing Through Lilliputian Eyes

Students apply their knowledge of scale and measurement systems to determine whether headlines using the metric system could be true or are unbelievable. To demonstrate their knowledge, they write a story set in Lilliput and include a conversation that compares sizes in Lilliput and Ourland. Students summarize the 1-D, 2-D, and 3-D measurements of the objects they included in their stories and describe the strategies they used to determine the sizes of Lilliputian objects.

Mathematical Goals

- Measure and estimate lengths of objects using different measurement systems.
- Rescale objects using scale factors in different measurement systems.
- Calculate linear measurement with fractions.
- Demonstrate an increased understanding of area and volume.
- Incorporate accurate size information into stories.
- Communicate mathematical ideas in a story.

MATERIALS

PER STUDENT

- Reproducibles R6, R19, R21

PER GROUP

- yardstick, tape measure, or string

5

Determining a Scale Factor Less Than One

I had my students discuss what measurements they found for the tracings. When students' answers differed, I asked them to describe exactly how they measured each tracing. My goal was for students to recognize that measurements can be made with different degrees of accuracy and that the same object can be measured in different ways. Some students measured to the nearest nearest $\frac{1}{16}$ inch, while others rounded up or down to the nearest $\frac{1}{4}$ inch. I found that some of my students measured from different starting points, such as measuring an arm by starting at the shoulder vs. starting at the underarm. □

Sizing Up the Lilliputians

Have students review the phase overview on pages 288–289 in the Student Guide.

1 Finding Clues in the Story

After students have read Gulliver's journal entries in the Phase Two introduction, Student Guide page 288, and this lesson, discuss with them how Gulliver's size compares to the sizes of things in the land of Lilliput.

- How does Gulliver's size compare to the sizes of objects in the land of Lilliput? Give examples.

- How do you think sizes of things in Lilliput would compare to sizes of things in Brobdingnag?

Gulliver towers above the people, animals, and houses in Lilliput. Help students to understand that by comparing Lilliput to Ourland, they are considering scale factors that make objects smaller, rather than larger.

You may want to have students use the scale factor for Brobdingnag in a sentence and relate it to the ratio (12:1). For example, "An object in Brobdingnag is 12 times larger than the same object in Ourland." Have students estimate the scale factor for Lilliput and use the scale factor in a similar sentence. You may decide to use any scale factor around 1:10 or 1:12 for the activities in this phase. For clarity, all solutions provided here assume a scale factor of 1:12. If another scale factor is used, answers will vary accordingly.

2 Looking for Clues to Determine a Scale Factor

The clues that students used to determine the scale factor for Brobdingnag were all found in the text of the journal entries. Most of the clues needed to determine the scale factor for Lilliput are found in the tracings. Make sure students recognize that the tracings show the actual sizes of people, animals, and objects in Lilliput. As students identify size clues in both the written text and the sketches of the journal, they will begin to see a relationship between the sizes of things in Lilliput and Ourland.

Students should carefully measure all aspects of the tracings—length and width, down to the fraction of an inch. Accurate measurement is essential to student success in the following steps.

hot topics

- *Size and Scale (8•6)*
  Exercises 4,7

Object	Lilliput Scale Size	Ourland Actual Size
an	6 inches	
ep	7 inches	72 inches
os	1½ inches	84 inches
dent	3 inches	18 inches
print	4½ inches	36 inches
print	½ inches	54 inches
master	1 inche	6 inches
als	6 inches	12 inches
	½ inch	72 inches
lip	3½ inches	6 inches
aser		42 inches
s		3 inches
		½ inch
		5 inches

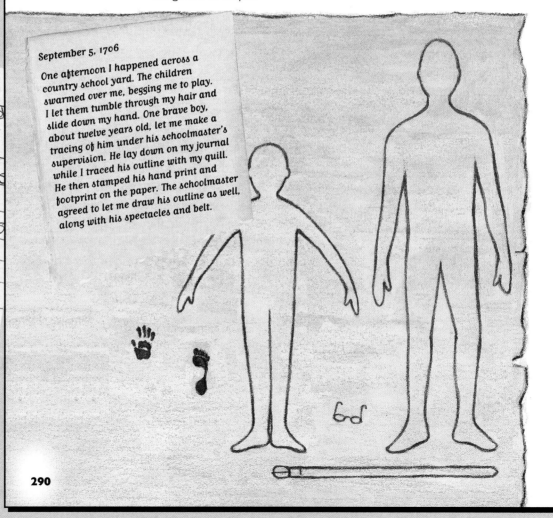

5 Sizing Up the Lilliputians

DETERMINING
A SCALE FACTOR
LESS THAN ONE

Gulliver is swept overboard in a storm at sea and wakes up in a new land. He is the captive of tiny people in the land of Lilliput. How are the sizes of things in Lilliput related to sizes in Ourland? Clues in the journal will help you find out how small things are in Lilliput.

September 5, 1706

One afternoon I happened across a country school yard. The children swarmed over me, begging me to play. I let them tumble through my hair and slide down my hand. One brave boy, about twelve years old, let me make a tracing of him under his schoolmaster's supervision. He lay down on my journal while I traced his outline with my quill. He then stamped his hand print and footprint on the paper. The schoolmaster agreed to let me draw his outline as well, along with his spectacles and belt.

290

Many students used the proportions of their own bodies and the Lilliputian tracings to estimate the sizes of other things in Lilliput:

"My desk is about an arm's length from the ground. The length of the Lilliputian child's arm is about $1\frac{3}{4}$ inches, so I estimated the desk is $1\frac{3}{4}$ inches high. But when I checked it with the scale factor—it didn't add up—the desk should have been bigger. This made me think that maybe the Lilliputian student was short for his age, or maybe my scale factor was wrong." ☐

My class discovered that in their Student Guides the Ourland size was always listed second in a scale factor. As a class, we established this convention for whenever we discussed or wrote the scale factor. That made it possible to quickly see whether the Ourland size was bigger or smaller than the size in the other land, and helped students communicate scale factors without confusion. ☐

3 Creating a Chart to Compare Sizes

To create a chart that compares sizes, students should begin by using the first column of the chart to write in the Lilliputian measurements described or traced in the journal. They can work individually or in groups to measure or estimate the size of comparable objects from Ourland. They should then add the measurements to their charts in the Ourland column to determine the scale factor, which is approximately 1:12. You may want to stop at this point to discuss the different scale factors or come to consensus as a class.

To complete their individual charts, students should choose at least four objects that they can measure in the classroom and four objects from outside the classroom. They should estimate or measure the Ourland size of each object and use the scale factor to calculate the size of the object in Lilliput. Let students know that they will be creating a scale drawing of one of these objects later, as part of Lesson 6.

It is important that students use a combination of measurements from all of the tracings to determine the scale factor because later in this lesson it is discovered that the student shown in the tracing is smaller in scale size than an average student.

An Answer Key for items 1–2 can be found on Assessment page A22.

4 Finding Average Sizes

Students can work individually or in groups to investigate the mean and median heights of their classmates. Next, they should use the scale factor to calculate the average height of a Lilliputian student and add it to their charts. As students compare the average Lilliputian height to the height of the tracing, encourage them to review their Lilliput Scale Chart to see if any other measurements (average handprint or footprint, desk, etc.) should be added or changed to reflect the average height. You may also want to prompt students to apply their knowledge of fractions with additional questions:

- What fraction of one's height is taken up by the length of the legs? by the torso? by the head?

- How does arm length relate to height? How does hand length relate to arm length?

5 Writing About Estimation Strategies

After students have completed their charts, have them describe in writing the different strategies they used for figuring out the sizes of objects from Ourland and Lilliput. Encourage students to include their discoveries about ways to find the average size of an object.

DO THE STUDENTS' CHARTS AND WRITING SHOW:

- *correct measurements of actual-size objects?*
- *effective estimation strategies?*
- *correct calculations to rescale objects?*
- *understanding of mean size and proportion?*

See *Gulliver's Worlds* Assessment page A9 for assessment information.

Glum-gluffs

We took a ruler and drew a line equal to 1 inch and divided it into 12 parts to make a Lilliputian ruler. We then measured things in Ourland with our an Ourland ruler and then used the Lilliputian ruler to find out how big the same thing would be in Ourland. For example, the computer screen in Ourland is 3/4 inches wide. We marked 10 and 3/4 on Lilliputian ruler to show the size of a ...uter screen there.

Create a Chart to Compare Sizes

Make a scale chart with three columns. Column 1 is for the name of an object. Column 2 is for the size of the object in Lilliput. Column 3 is for the size in Ourland. Use a ruler to measure the tracings.

1 Use the words and tracings in the story to record the name of the object and its Lilliputian measurements on the chart. Measure or estimate the size of the same object in Ourland.

2 Use the information in your scale chart to find a scale factor that shows how sizes in Lilliput are related to sizes in Ourland.

3 Estimate or measure the sizes of some more objects in Ourland. Add these objects and their Ourland measurements to the chart. Find the size each object would be in Lilliput and add that information to the chart.

Do you think the Lilliputian student in the tracing is tall, short, or average-size in a Lilliputian sixth-grade class?

Write About Estimation Strategies

Write about what you did and learned as you investigated sizes of things in Lilliput.

- Describe the measurement and estimation strategies you used to find the sizes of things in Ourland and Lilliput. Show how you used the scale factor to complete your chart.

- What did you discover about finding the average size of an object?

How are sizes of things in Lilliput related to sizes in Ourland?

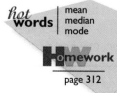

hot words | mean
median
mode

Homework

page 312

Glum-gluffs and Mum-gluffs

To help those students who needed language support, I brought the actual toys described in the journal (doll, wagon) into the classroom. As a class we put the doll into the wagon and estimated how many "men" would fit in each boat. My class found that the wagon was a too small to be accurately compared to a ship and estimated that a wheelbarrow would be closer to scale. □

Students found that 1 glum-gluff is about ¾ of an inch, or about 2 centimeters. Many students ended up making rulers that had all three measurement systems on it: Lilliputian, U.S., and metric. I encouraged them to include their rulers in their portfolios. □

1 Discussing Measurement Systems

After students have read Gulliver's journal, have them compare how things are measured in Lilliput to the U.S. customary system and the metric system. You can help students visualize the scenes in the journal by relating the sizes of various objects described in the journal to objects in the classroom. Discuss what the measurements of those classroom objects would be in customary units and in metric units.

- Can you find something in the classroom that is about 1 centimeter in length?

- Can you find something in the classroom that is about 1 meter in length?

- How would you describe the same objects using the U.S. customary system?

- What object in the classroom is about the size of a Lilliputian ship? How could you describe its measurements using the U.S. customary and metric systems?

You may need to review with students the relationship between the U.S. customary units of inches, feet, and yards: there are 12 inches in a foot and 3 feet in a yard. Students may be less familiar with the relationship between the centimeter and meter in the metric system: there are 100 centimeters in a meter. The U.S. customary system is sometimes called the English system, but will be consistently referred to as the U.S. customary system in this unit.

2 Investigating Nonstandard Measurement Units

To help students see the relationship between the Lilliputian units mum-gluff and glum-gluff mentioned in Gulliver's journal, have them measure the tracing of a glum-gluff found on the journal page. Ask them to create a ruler that is a mum-gluff long (20 glum-gluffs). When students have created the ruler, have them use it to draw outlines, or tracings, of the king and queen, based on information found in the journal entry. Tell students to label the measurements in both mum-gluffs and inches.

homework options

LESSON HOMEWORK

Page 313

hot topics

• *Systems of Measurement (8•1)
  Exercises 1–7*

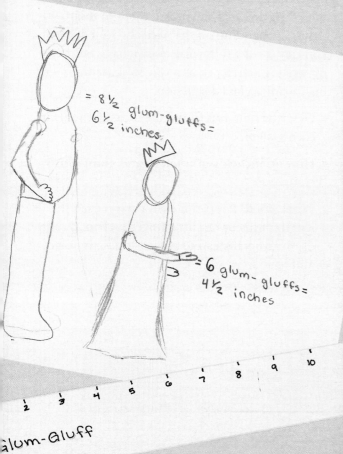

= 8½ glum-gluffs
6½ inches=

= 6 glum-gluffs
4½ inches

glum-gluff

6 Glum-gluffs and Mum-gluffs

MEASURING WITH
NONSTANDARD
UNITS

The same object can be measured in different units of measurement. Inches and feet are units in the U.S. customary system of measurement. Centimeters and meters are units in the metric system. How do these units compare to the units used in Lillilput?

October 5, 1706

During dinner, the King and Queen told stories about their country and people, and I told stories of mine. The King found it especially hard to believe that he, one of the tallest men in his land, would be no bigger than a child's doll in mine. He informed me that he was 8½ slum-gluffs tall, and that the Queen was 6 slum-gluffs tall. When I inquired what a slum-gluff was, he replied that it was $\frac{1}{20}$ of a mum-gluff. He then kindly agreed to have his steward mark the length of 1 slum-gluff in my journal.

———— 1 slum-gluff

292

Students had various strategies for finding things in Ourland that were the same size as things in Lilliput:

"I cut a string the length of the Lilliputian adult tracing. I used the string to find objects that were about the same size in Ourland." □

Before we began the discussion, we took a vote as a class to see which was the "best" measurement system. Overwhelmingly, students preferred the U.S. customary system. I then had the class break into groups of four and use their scale drawings to answer the discussion questions. As students were asked to justify their choices, they began to see that different systems are appropriate for different tasks. A later class vote showed the metric system to be the favorite for this activity. Lynn made an interesting point:

"If you use a scale of 1:12, the customary system is easier, since you can just change feet to inches. But if you use a scale of 1:10, then the metric system is easier because it is a base-ten system." □

student page

3 Measuring an Object in Different Systems

Before students begin this step, make sure they are comfortable with the standard units in the U.S. customary system and the metric system, and that they have a good sense of the nonstandard Lilliputian units. As students select and draw one object from their charts from Lesson 5, point out that the measurements they are using are U.S. customary units. They will need to use a metric ruler to measure their scale drawings in metric units and they will need the rulers they created in Step 2 to measure the drawings in nonstandard Lilliputian units.

student page

4 Comparing Measurement Systems

When students have finished labeling their drawings with glum-gluffs, inches, and centimeters and have identified an object in Ourland that would be about the same size, have them write a letter describing how they chose appropriate measurement units for a particular task. Encourage students to use their scale drawings to support their answers and attach them to their letters. Depending on the needs of your students, you can use the following questions as either a prewriting activity or as a way to share their writing during a class discussion.

- Describe how you found the measurements in each system.

- How do inches, centimeters, and glum-gluffs compare?

- What would happen if each person used the length of his or her little finger or arm as units of measure, instead of measuring with inches and feet?

what to look for

DO THE STUDENTS' DRAWINGS AND LETTERS REFLECT:

- *an ability to accurately measure objects in standard and nonstandard units?*
- *an ability to rescale objects using a scale factor and estimation strategies?*
- *a clear description and evaluation of the U.S. customary and metric systems of measurement?*

See *Gulliver's Worlds* Assessment page A9 for assessment information.

Dear Highnesses,

When you look at my drawings, remember that
en you measure with the US. customary system, you
ld use feet and inches. There are 12 inches to a foot
three feet to a yard. There about 15 glum-gluffs in a

an also use the metric system to measure things.
tric uses centimeters and meters. There are 100
rs to a meter. A glum-gluff is about 2 cm.

you should use the metric system to measure
illiput, because when I measured with inches I
h of fractions because the objects were to

Measure an Object in Different Systems

Choose an object that you added to the Lilliput scale chart you made in Lesson 5.

1 Use the measurements recorded in the chart to make an accurate, life-size drawing of the object in Lilliput.

2 Use a metric ruler to measure the drawing in metric units (centimeters). Write the metric measurements on the drawing.

3 Calculate what the measurements of the drawing would be in the Lilliputian units of glum-gluffs. Write the Lilliputian measurements on the drawing.

4 Compare the object in the drawing to any object in Ourland that would be about the same size. Write the name of the Ourland object on the drawing.

> **How do the units used in different measurement systems compare?**

Compare Measurement Systems

Write a letter to the King and Queen of Lilliput. Compare the measurement systems of Ourland and Lilliput. Make sure your letter answers the following questions:

- When would you prefer to use the U.S. customary system of measurement? When would you prefer to use the metric system?

- Would you ever prefer to use glum-gluffs and mum-gluffs? Why?

- Suppose the people in Lilliput were going to adopt one of our measurement systems. Which one would you recommend to them? Why or why not?

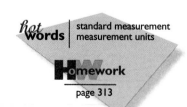

hot **words** | standard measurement
measurement units

Homework
page 313

GULLIVER'S WORLDS • LESSON 6   293

7

LESSON

Solving Problems Involving Area and Volume

Some of my students needed to be reminded about the differences among area, volume, and linear measurement, while others were ready to take the next step. I encouraged students who needed a challenge to devise a formula to determine how many mattresses would be needed to make Gulliver comfortable and to explain how it worked during the discussion. □

Housing and Feeding Gulliver

1 Exploring Area and Volume in Stories

As students read Gulliver's journal, have them focus on the problem of how the Lilliputians could possibly house and feed Gulliver. Encourage students to substitute their favorite foods for the bread, meat, and cider. Have them estimate how much food they would need to eat a filling lunch in Lilliput.

- What did you estimate for the amount of Lilliputian bread you would need to eat for lunch? How did you determine that amount?

- What did you estimate for drink? Explain your reasoning.

2 Discussing Area and Volume

Have students visualize the individual objects mentioned in the journal and estimate how many of those objects Gulliver would need. Encourage students to go beyond the idea that the scale factor is approximately 12:1 and imagine the object in three dimensions. Students should start to connect how many Lilliputian mattresses it would take to cover an Ourland mattress with the term area, and how many mattresses it would take to fill the mattress with the term volume. You may want to discuss the following points to prepare students for the next step.

- If the Lilliputians gave Gulliver 12 mattresses, what would his bed look like?

- If they gave him 144 mattresses, he could arrange them in a 12 × 12 rectangle, but would the bed be comfortable for him?

At the end of the discussion, you may want to share with students the fact that in the original story, about 600 mattresses were used to produce a bed for Gulliver. Even then, he did not find the bed as soft and comfortable as he would have liked. Perhaps these were arranged as 12 × 12 × 4, which would require 576 mattresses.

hot **topics**

- *Volume (7•7)*
  Exercises 1–5

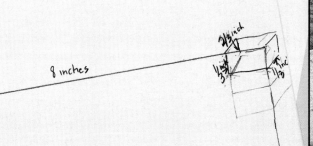

I figured out the size of lilliputian loaves of bread by multiplying the leanth the Wepth and the Hight of a regular size of bread.

I built my model by cutting do.

...zes to fit the right l...

...pth.

...fferent

8 inches

7 Housing and Feeding Gulliver

SOLVING PROBLEMS
INVOLVING AREA
AND VOLUME

Gulliver's needs for food and shelter in Lilliput present some interesting problems. These problems involve area and volume. In the last phase, you solved problems in one dimension. Now you will extend your work with the Lilliputian scale factor to solve problems in two and three dimensions.

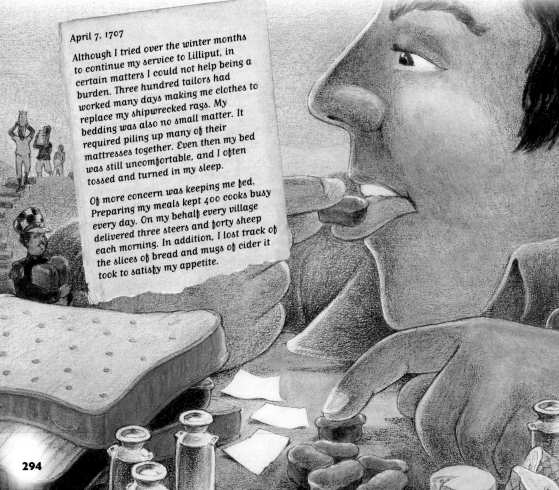

April 7, 1707

Although I tried over the winter months to continue my service to Lilliput, in certain matters I could not help being a burden. Three hundred tailors had worked many days making me clothes to replace my shipwrecked rags. My bedding was also no small matter. It required piling up many of their mattresses together. Even then my bed was still uncomfortable, and I often tossed and turned in my sleep.

Of more concern was keeping me fed. Preparing my meals kept 400 cooks busy every day. On my behalf every village delivered three steers and forty sheep each morning. In addition, I lost track of the slices of bread and mugs of cider it took to satisfy my appetite.

294

This investigation held real mathematical surprises for students. In several cases, students arrived at correct answers but rejected them because they could not believe that Gulliver could eat so many Lilliputian loaves of bread, or would need so many mattresses to make a bed. This was a good lead-in to considering 1, 2, and 3 dimensions, and what happens when you take the square and cube of a number. ☐

I assigned one scale model to each member of the group, so that within each group we had a physical model for each object. In several cases, making the scale models made students see that their answers were not correct— most of the time this was because they were not thinking about all three dimensions. ☐

student page

3 Estimating to Solve Area and Volume Problems

Have students estimate the number of Lilliputian objects needed by Gulliver. Students should consider not only the area of the object, but also the volume. At this point, you may want to introduce or review the notes contrasting linear measurement (one dimension), area measurement (two dimensions: length and width) and volume measurement (three dimensions: length, width, and height) from Lesson 3, page 285A.

For the first question, a volume problem, students could imagine a 10-row by 10-column arrangement of Lilliputian mattresses stacked in 10 layers. In the second question, where thickness is not involved, 100 sheets of Lilliputian paper in a 10-by-10 arrangement would make a suitable sheet of writing paper for Gulliver. That is, powers of 10 suggest appropriate magnitudes for students' responses to these questions. Question 3 is a volume problem with an additional factor of 2; Gulliver might need 2,000 loaves of bread per week. Question 4 implies a factor of $\frac{3}{4}$ or 0.75: there are 4 cups in a quart and Gulliver drinks 3 cups per day; $0.75 \times 10^3 = 750$.

student page

4 Using a Model to Check an Estimate

Have students work individually or in groups to construct a actual-size model of one of the Lilliputian objects. Make sure that they measure accurately and that they think about all three dimensions. Students should use the Lilliputian model to demonstrate that their solution to the problem is correct. Encourage students to describe how they checked their answers verbally or in writing.

what to look for

Estimate to Solve Area and Volume Problems

Estimate how many of the Lilliputian objects Gulliver needs. Then make a Lilliputian-size model of one of the four objects.

1 How many Lilliputian-size mattresses would Gulliver need to make a bed? How should Gulliver arrange those mattresses to make a comfortable-size bed?

2 How many sheets of Lilliputian paper would need to be taped together to made one sheet of writing paper for Gulliver?

3 At home, Gulliver would eat two loaves of bread each week. How many Lilliputian loaves of bread would Gulliver need each week?

4 At home, Gulliver drank 3 cups of milk each day. How many Lilliputian-size quarts of milk would Gulliver need each day?

> How can you use estimation to solve problems in two and three dimensions?

Use a Model to Check an Estimate

Describe in writing how you can use your Lilliputian-size model to check your estimate. Include a sketch with measurements to show your thinking.

hot **words** | volume

H♦**mework**
page 314

Writing About Area and Volume

I had my students secretly choose objects from their backpacks. I then had them try to "see" those objects through the eyes of a Lilliputian. My students found that they had to think in three dimensions and visualize the objects from lots of different angles to truly grasp their sizes in Lilliput. □

For some students Metric Headlines was too simple. I added the option of translating the headlines into U.S. customary and Lilliputian measurements to give them more of a challenge. □

Seeing Through Lilliputian Eyes

1 Visualizing in One, Two, and Three Dimensions

When students have finished reading this final entry of Gulliver's journal, have them work in groups to figure out what objects from Gulliver's pocket the Lilliputians were describing. After students have guessed what each object might be, have the groups share their guesses. You can then reveal that the objects mentioned in the journal are, respectively, a handkerchief, a writing journal, a comb, some coins, and a pocket watch.

A good writing extension is to have each student choose one object from his or her backpack or pocket and describe it in Lilliputian terms. Students can exchange their descriptions with a partner and guess what each other's object is.

2 Evaluating the Accuracy of Metric Measurements

Remind students how they evaluated different headlines using the U.S. customary system in Lesson 4. Pass out the Metric Headlines, Reproducible R21, and have students determine whether each statement is believable. To save time, you may assign this step as homework.

This activity extends the previous Headlines investigation from Lesson 4 to include two and three dimensions. You may want to point out that comparisons between different Lilliputian objects and Ourland objects involve covering or filling to get at area and volume.

An Answer Key for Reproducible R21 can be found on Assessment page A22.

homework options

LESSON HOMEWORK

Page 315

hot topics

- *Addition and Subtraction of Fractions (2•3)*
  Exercises 1–9
- *Multiplication and Division of Fractions (2•4)*
  Exercises 1–4, 18–21

Metric Headlines

a. I saw a Lilliputian house that was 15 cm tall and 25 cm wide.

b. I could carry a Lilliputian car in my pocket

c. I saw a Lilliputian house that could fit in my lunch box

I saw a Lilliputian Elephant that was 30 cm tall

I saw a Lilliputian foot ball field that was the size of an Ourland Door mat

saw a Lilliputian door that was the size of Ourland Postage Stamp

ld grow 5 Lilliputian Door that was the f an Ourland Postage Stamp

w a Lilliput Mountain that was 40 's tall

8 Seeing Through Lilliputian Eyes

WRITING ABOUT AREA AND VOLUME

Imagine yourself in Lilliput. What objects would you bring with you? How would the Lilliputians describe these objects? You will use what you have learned about scale in one, two, and three dimensions when you write a story describing your own adventures in Lilliput.

Gulliver's Pocket Contents:

1. One great piece of coarse cloth, large enough to be a carpet for your Majesty's chief Room of State
2. A great bundle of white thin substances, folded one over another, about the thickness of three men, tied with a strong cable and marked with black figures, with every letter almost half as large as the palm of our hands
3. A long pole from the back of which extended 20 shorter poles, resembling the palace railings
4. Several round flat pieces of yellow and silver metal, of different bulk, some so large and heavy that my comrade and I could hardly lift them
5. Some wonderful kind of globe-like engine, part silver and part transparent metal, with a loud noise like the sound of a water-mill, attached by a great silver chain

296

My students were really interested in reading the complete Gulliver story. I found that there were several versions of Gulliver's Travels *that were easier to read and more age-appropriate than the original Jonathan Swift satire. I found two great versions of the complete Gulliver story on tape. One is narrated by Joel Grey and the other by Hugh Laurie. In addition, there are several movies available on video:* Gulliver's Travels *(1939, 1977, 1996),* The Three Worlds of Gulliver *(1960) and* Gulliver Mickey *(1934).* □

student page

3 Writing a Story Using 3-D Measurements

Students may notice that this investigation is similar to the one in Lesson 4, but this time they will write a story that describes the different objects in three dimensions using different measurement systems. Students should include a conversation with a Lilliputian that compares at least one object in Lilliput to an object in Ourland. Encourage students to explore volume and area relationships in their conversations by asking the following questions:

- How many Lilliputian versions of an object would it take to cover an Ourland version of the object? (area)

- How many Lilliputian versions of an object would it take to fill an Ourland object? (volume)

student page

4 Describing Rescaling Strategies

Have students prepare short summaries that can be used to assess growth in their understanding of area and volume relationships. In their writing, students should focus on how they determined the length, width, and height of their objects and how the objects compared to objects in Ourland. You may want to have them reflect on their Lesson 4 summaries and describe what new things they learned in this phase about scale, proportion, and measurement.

- *estimate or measure length, width, and height accurately?*
- *describe measurements using different systems?*
- *rescale in 1, 2, and 3 dimensions with accurate computations?*
- *describe their strategies clearly?*

See *Gulliver's Worlds* Assessment pages A10–A11 for assessment information.

ADDITIONAL assessment O p t i o n s

- **Assessment Rubric,** page A11

- **Phase Two Student Assessment Criteria,** page R6

- **Phase Two Skill Quiz,** page R3

- **Phase Two Skill Quiz Answers,** page A12

Write a Story Using 3-D Measurements

Write a believable story using three-dimensional measurements. You will need to figure out the correct length, width, and height of the objects you describe.

1 Imagine a place in Lilliput. Describe at least one adventure that could happen to you there.

2 Describe the measurements of at least three objects found in the place. You could include an Ourland object in your story for comparison.

3 Include a conversation with a Lilliputian that compares the sizes of the objects in the story to the same objects in Ourland.

4 Record and check all of your measurements.

Describe Rescaling Strategies

Summarize how you determined the length, width, and height of the three objects described in your story.

- Make a table, list, or drawing showing the length, width, and height of each object in both Ourland and Lilliput.

- Explain the methods you used to estimate or measure each object. Show how you rescaled it using the scale factor.

How can you describe a three-dimensional Lilliputian world?

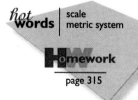

hot **words** | scale metric system

Homework
page 315

September 13, 1708

It has now been some months since my journal was published. News of my travels has prompted a greater response than I expected. I must confess, too, a certain pleasure at the attentions I have received from my publisher. He has pronounced himself well-pleased with the sales figures, and credits both my nature and my writing for this success.

Although I did not anticipate it, I have recently received much correspondence from my readers. Pictures and letters have come from nearby countries—France, Spain and Holland—as well as more distant lands. It is my dream that someday all my treasures and adventures may be shared with the public as part of a glorious exhibit, but, alas, I fear it will not happen in my lifetime.

Your friend,

Lemuel Gulliver

Welcome to our BIGVILLE dinner party

PHASE THREE

Further Explorations of Scale Factors

In this final phase, students work with a variety of scale factors. Scale factors from Lesson 9, Lands of the Large, enlarge objects; scale factors from Lesson 10, Lands of the Little, shrink objects. Building on the first two phases, the scales are now more complex, represented with decimals (e.g., 4.5:1; 0.375:1), fractions (e.g., $4\frac{1}{2}$:1; $\frac{3}{8}$:1), or integers greater than 1 (e.g., 9:2; 3:8).

Students also compare size relationships across the lands. For example, if the scale factor relating Maximar to Brobdingnag is 1:4 and the scale factor relating Upscale to Maximar is 1:2, what scale factor relates Upscale to Brobdingnag? Some students will solve these problems by creating sample objects from each land and comparing their sizes; others will use sketches or simple models; and others will compute the answers (e.g., $\frac{1}{4} \times \frac{1}{2} = \frac{1}{8}$, so the scale factor is 1:8).

More on Area and Volume

In Lesson 11, students look more systematically at the effect of rescaling on area and volume. Starting with a small cube, they make large cubes at scale factors ranging from 2 to 25 and record the number of small cubes needed to match the length of one size, the area of one face, and the volume of the whole enlarged cube. Their data will show that in every case length changes by the scale factor, area by the square of the scale factor, and volume by the cube of the scale factor.

As shown in the Math Background for Phase Two, if the scale factor is 4, we would need to arrange the original cubes into a 4 by 4 square to cover the area of one side of the enlarged cube. Volume adds a third dimension; we would need 4 layers of this arrangement to match the volume of the enlarged cube.

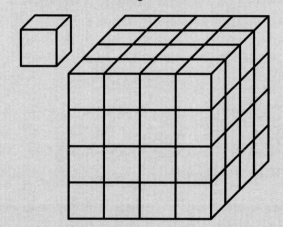

Imagine you are in charge of a special exhibit about *Gulliver's Worlds*. How would you show the sizes of the different lands he visited? In this final phase, you will explore size relationships in different lands, both big and small. You will find ways to show how the sizes compare in length, area, and volume. Finally, your class will create displays of life-size objects from one of *Gulliver's Worlds*.

Lands of the Large and Lands of the Little

WHAT'S THE MATH?

Investigations in this section focus on:

DATA COLLECTION
- Gathering information from pictures
- Creating displays to show size relationships

MEASUREMENT and ESTIMATION
- Measuring accurately using fractions
- Exploring area and volume measurements

SCALE and PROPORTION
- Finding scale factors that describe relationships among sizes
- Enlarging and reducing the sizes of objects according to scale factors
- Creating 2-D scale drawings
- Creating a 3-D scale model
- Exploring the effects of rescaling on area and volume

MathScape Online
mathscape1.com/self_check_quiz

AT A GLANCE

LESSON 9

Lands of the Large

Students analyze pictures from different Lands of the Large to determine the scale factor of each land. They investigate proportional relationships within one scale by working together to create an actual-size face from one of the lands. Students use both integer and noninteger scale factors to sketch faces from different lands and then present their sketches in a chart to show size relationships between different scales.

Mathematical Goals

- Rescale using integer and noninteger scale factors.
- Create scale drawings.
- Examine proportional relationships.
- Represent size relationships.

MATERIALS

PER GROUP

- pencils, markers, or crayons
- ruler
- scissors
- glue or tape
- large sheet of paper

LESSON 10

Lands of the Little

Students evaluate sketches from different Lands of the Little to see if the scale factor is correct. Then they work in groups to correct the sketches. Students create a comparison chart that shows how the sizes of things in Ourland compare to the sizes of things in Lands of the Little and write a guide showing how the chart can predict the size of an object in each land.

Mathematical Goals

- Rescale using integer and noninteger scale factors.
- Use scale factors less than one, which reduce the size of the original.
- Compare and analyze size relationships among several lands.
- Develop strategies for predicting the sizes of objects in different lands.
- Communicate mathematical information with diagrams and words.

MATERIALS

PER GROUP

- pencils, markers or crayons
- paper (snapshot size)
- ruler

PER STUDENT

- ruler
- large sheet of paper

LESSON 11

Gulliver's Worlds Cubed

Students use cubes to examine patterns in linear, area, and volume measurements. Starting with a small cube, students build models of it in different scales and then determine how many of the original cubes they would need to cover and fill each of the rescaled cubes. Student create a chart and analyze the number patterns to generate rules for predicting area and volume measurements in different scales.

Mathematical Goals

- Create 3-D scale models.

- Formulate rules to predict area and volume measurements.

- Apply exponents to measurement units to describe area and volume.

- Compare the effect of rescaling on linear, area, and volume measurements.

MATERIALS

PER GROUP

- graph paper

- 50–100 Rainbow Centimeter Cubes (optional)

LESSON 12

Stepping into Gulliver's Worlds

Students create a display of one of Gulliver's Worlds for a museum in the classroom. They create life-size objects and write a guidebook that describes and compares the sizes of objects in the display. As each display is presented, visitors to the museum check for accurate information about the length, area, and volume measurements of the objects in the displays. Students evaluate their own displays and reflect on their learning from the entire unit.

Mathematical Goals

- Creating accurate 3-D scale models.

- Estimate and measure length, width, and height.

- Describe measurements using different systems and exponents.

- Communicate mathematical information with words and diagrams.

MATERIALS

PER STUDENT

- ruler or tape measure

- Reproducibles R6, R22, R23

PER GROUP

- art materials (optional)

9

Representing Size Relationships

The class came up with three different ways to represent scale when it wasn't a simple "integer to 1" relationship. Some used fractions, some decimals, and some changed it to an integer relationship. In Behemoth, for example, the three ways to write the scale would be 4.5 to 1, 4½ to 1, and 9 to 2. □

I passed out pieces of white construction paper to each group for the different facial features. I then had students glue their pieces onto one piece of butcher paper and present it to the class using the face as a mask. The students really liked making the heads, and several used them as models for their final project in Lesson 12. □

Lands of the Large

Have students review the phase overview on pages 298–299 in the Student Guide.

student page

1 Comparing Sizes of Objects from Different Lands

In this lesson, students work together as a class to create the Lands of the Large display. As they work individually or with a partner to examine the photographs of an Ourland object next to a Lands of the Large object, Student Guide page 300, they determine the scale factor for each land.

👉 You may need to point out that the smaller object is always from Ourland and that some of the scale factors use nonintegers. You may want to begin the activity by examining the photograph from Gargantua as a class and helping students discover that the scale factor can be described using fractions, decimals, or integers: 7.5:1, $7\frac{1}{2}$ to 1, or 15:2.

> Possible scale factors can be found on Assessment page A23.

2 Investigating Proportions of Faces

After students have checked that their scale factors are correct, have them form groups of four or five and assign each group a different Land of the Large. Have students work together to assemble a life-size face for their group's land. Each student should make a sketch of one facial feature. Then the group puts the features together in realistic combinations. This activity is self-checking. If students have measured and rescaled carefully, everything should look in proportion when they put the pieces together.

homework options

LESSON HOMEWORK

Page 316

*hot*topics

• *Fraction, Decimal, and Percent Relationships (2•9)*
  Exercises 1–30

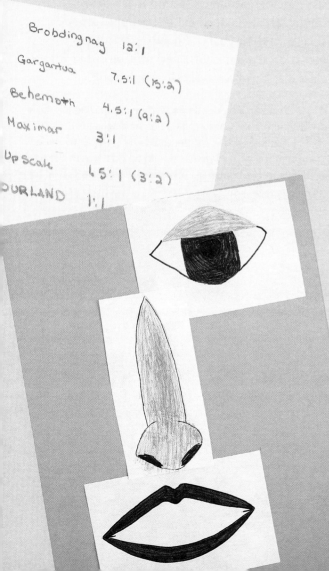

Brobdingnag   12:1

Gargantua   7.5:1 (15:2)

Behemoth   4.5:1 (9:2)

Maximar   3:1

Upscale   1.5:1 (3:2)

OURLAND   1:1

9 Lands of the Large

REPRESENTING SIZE
RELATIONSHIPS

Ourland Museum needs a display that compares the sizes of objects from Lands of the Large to Ourland.
Can you figure out the scale factor for each of the Lands of the Large? Can you find a way to show the size relationships among the different lands?

Investigate Proportions of Faces

How large is a life-size face in each of the Lands of the Large?

Compare the objects in the photos to find the scale factor. The smaller object is always from Ourland. When you are finished, check to make sure your scale factor is correct before you do the following group investigation.

1 As a group, select one of the Lands of the Large for this investigation. Have each member of your group draw a different feature of a face from your group's land.

2 As a group, arrange the features to form a realistic face. Check to see if your measurements are correct and the features are in proportion. Work together to draw the outline of the face.

How tall would a person in your group's Land of the Large be?

Gargantua

Behemoth

Upscale

Maximar

300 **GULLIVER'S WORLDS** • LESSON 9

I had students create a "life-size" display on the wall to compare the group faces before I had them make the scale drawings and charts. I had a student from the class stand in for the Ourland face. When we looked for size relationships as a class, many students were able to see the connections of Maximar being $\frac{1}{4}$ the size of Brobdingnag and Upscale being half of Maximar. I referred back to the wall chart for Step 5 when we looked at lands in comparison to Brobdingnag. □

To find the scale factor of their land to Brobdingnag some students used the decimal scale factors from Ourland and divided. For example, Brobdingnag to Ourland is 12:1 and Gargantua to Ourland is 7.5:1. The scale factor for Brobdingnag to Gargantua is 12 to 7.5, or 12:7.5, and 7.5 ÷ 12 = 0.62. Students could then see that things in Gargantua were about $\frac{2}{3}$ the size of things in Brobdingnag. □

3 Discussing Size Relationships from Other Lands

As the groups share their Lands of the Large faces with the class, encourage students to compare the size of each face to the size of their own faces and look for size relationships. You may want to ask the following questions to help students compare sizes:

- What is the largest face? the smallest?

- How many Maximar faces tall is a Brobdingnag face?

- How many Upscale faces tall is a Maximar face?

- How many Maximar faces would it take to cover a Brobdingnag face?

- How can you tell if each part of the face has been rescaled correctly? What would it look like if the scale was wrong for the nose?

4 Representing Size Relationships

Refer students to the scale drawing of the Ourland face, Student Guide page 301, and have them make simple scale drawings of faces from each of the lands. As students organize their drawings into a display of size relationships, you may want to have them describe the size relationships to a partner or in writing.

Students should focus on sketching the relative sizes of the Lands of the Large heads compared to the Ourland scale drawing and not concern themselves with the scale factor of the drawing itself (1:12).

5 Describing a Scale Factor for Brobdingnag

Depending on time, students can either work individually or in groups to determine the scale factor for each land as compared to the sizes of things in Brobdingnag. Have students describe in writing how they used visualization, measurement, and calculations to determine the new scale factors. Students should mark the Brobdingnag scale factor next to the appropriate sketch on their charts. Encourage students to incorporate their charts and writing either into a class display or an individual notebook.

You can introduce this step by comparing the scale factors of Ourland (1:1), Brobdingnag (12:1), and Maximar (3:1). Students should be able to understand that things in Maximar would be one-fourth the size of things in Brobdingnag. Therefore, the scale factor for Maximar to Brobdingnag would be $\frac{1}{4}$ of 1 (1:4) or 0.25:1.

what to look for

DO THE STUDENTS' SKETCHES SHOW:

- *correct interpretation of integer and noninteger scale factors?*
- *accurate rescaling using scale factors?*
- *realistic proportional relationships?*
- *ability to determine size relationships (scale factors) in other lands?*

See *Gulliver's Worlds* Assessment page A13 for assessment information.

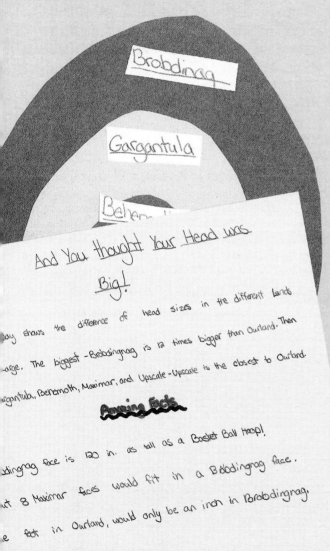

Represent Size Relationships

Use the scale drawing of an Ourland face on this page to make a simple scale drawing of a face from each of the Lands of the Large. Organize your drawings into a visual display to show size relationships.

1 Measure the scale drawing of the Ourland face.

2 Use the scale factors from the Lands of the Large to make a scale drawing of a face from each land. You do not need to draw in the features.

3 Write the name of the land and the scale factor compared to Ourland next to each drawing.

4 Organize your drawings into a display of size relationships that compares the sizes of faces from different lands and shows how they are related.

Describe a Scale Factor for Brobdingnag

Compare the sizes of things in each of the Lands of the Large to the sizes of things in Brobdingnag. Use this to explain how the scale factor describes size relationships.

- Figure out the scale factor for each land compared to Brobdingnag. Write it next to the scale drawing from that land.

- Describe in writing how you figured out the scale factor. Tell why it is different from the Ourland scale factor.

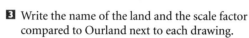

How do things in the Lands of the Large compare in size to things in Ourland?

hot **words** | picture graph

HW**omework**

page 316

10

Predicting
Scale Size

Some of my students had a hard time getting accurate measurements of the objects in the Lands of the Little scale drawings because some objects were so small. To help them, I used the xerox machine to enlarge the drawings 200%. It was also a nice concrete example of how the ratio remains the same even thought the measurements change. □

At first some students just concentrated on getting the height of each object right and sketched in the rest in their scale drawings. But they quickly discovered that their objects did not look well proportioned. This led them to measure the width of the objects as well as estimate the depth to get it to look right. □

Lands of
the Little

1 Checking the Sizes of Objects in Lands of the Little

In this lesson, students will work together as a class to correct and improve the existing Lands of the Little display at the Ourland Living Museum. Refer students to the scale drawings on Student Guide page 302 of an Ourland object next to a Lands of the Little object, and have them check whether the scale factor for each land matches the objects in the scale drawing. The larger object is always from Ourland. Remind students that they are looking for size relationships within the scale drawing and not the relationship between the drawing and life-size objects.

> The objects in the following scale drawings do not match the scale factor listed:

Small Town   2:3 (0.67:1)

Quarterville   1:4 (0.25:1)

2 Comparing Objects in the Lands of the Little

Have groups of five choose an Ourland object in the classroom and create a scale drawing of the object for each of the Lands of the Little. Each student should create one scale drawing for one assigned land. Then, as a group, they can organize their sketches to show size relationships. Encourage groups to check the length, width, and height measurements of the objects in each other's drawings.

> You may want to have students draw their Ourland objects with a height of 1 inch, 5 inches, or 10 inches to help them connect their drawings to the table in Step 3. Remind students that because they are making scale drawings and not life-size drawings, a television set in Ourland could be 1 inch tall as long as the size relationship between Ourland and Lilliput remains constant (a Lilliputian television would then be only $\frac{1}{12}$ of an inch tall).

LESSON HOMEWORK

Page 317

10 Lands of the Little

PREDICTING
SCALE SIZE

Can you find the mistakes in the Lands of the Little display? Here you will correct the scale drawings and create a chart that you can use to find the size of any object in a Land of the Little.

Compare Objects in the Lands of the Little

How do things in the Lands of the Little compare in size to things in Ourland?

Measure each pair of scale drawings on this page. The larger object is always from Ourland. Does the size relationship for each Land of the Little object match the scale factor below it?

1 As a group, choose an Ourland object from your classroom. Draw your object on a piece of paper.

2 Use each of the four scale factors below to draw a new picture of your object. Now, which scale drawings below do you think are incorrect?

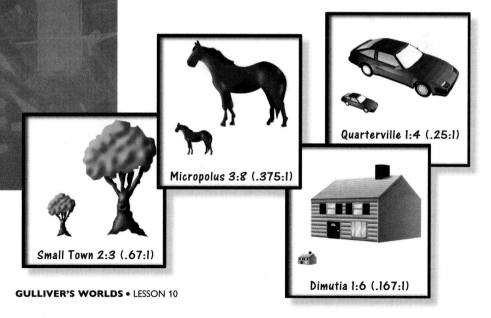

Quarterville 1:4 (.25:1)

Micropolus 3:8 (.375:1)

Small Town 2:3 (.67:1)

Dimutia 1:6 (.167:1)

I had my students take their tables home and share them with their parents. I encouraged them to have their parents add items to the chart. Students should then share with their parents how large that object would be in the various lands and how they figured it out. I received lots of good comments from parents, who were amazed at how quickly their child rescaled the objects. □

3 Creating a Table to Show Size Relationships

Students can work in groups or individually to make a table showing sizes in Ourland ranging from 100 inches to 1 inch or 10 inches. Have students list the corresponding sizes in the other lands for each Ourland object (10, 25, 50, 75, and 100). Students should be able to find an approximate size for an object from any land, given a size in another land, as long at the Ourland size is in the 100 to 10 range.

Some students may be ready to transform their tables into coordinate graphs. Help them to visualize how the numbers on their tables would look if they were plotted as coordinates and used to create separate lines for each land.

4 Writing a Guide for Using the Table

As students answer the questions, have them describe in writing the process they used to complete their table and how someone else could get information from it.

You may want to challenge some students to use their tables to predict measurements larger than the benchmarks by asking, "If an object is 200 inches long in Ourland, how can we use the table to find out how long it would be in other lands?"

An Answer Key can be found on Assessment page A23.

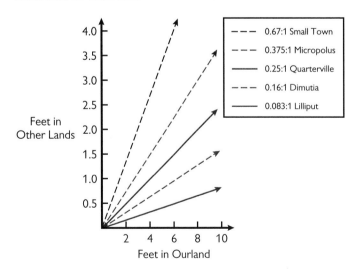

Legend:
- 0.67:1 Small Town
- 0.375:1 Micropolus
- 0.25:1 Quarterville
- 0.16:1 Dimutia
- 0.083:1 Lilliput

Y-axis: Feet in Other Lands
X-axis: Feet in Ourland

- *a comparison of size relationships among all lands?*
- *accurate calculations of measurements using scale factors?*
- *clear and logical instructions on how to use the table?*

See *Gulliver's Worlds* Assessment page A13 for assessment information.

Create a Table to Show Size Relationships

Make a table that shows how objects in the Lands of the Little compare in size to objects in Ourland. Record the size an object would be in other lands if you knew its size in Ourland.

1 Fill in the names of the Lands of the Little at the top of each column. Mark the Ourland measurements (100 inches, 75 inches, 50 inches, 25 inches, 10 inches) in the Ourland column.

2 Figure out how big an object would be in the Lands of the Little for each of the Ourland measurements. Mark the Lands of the Little measurements in the appropriate columns.

3 Find a way to use your group's scale drawings to check that your table is correct.

How could you show the size relationships of things in different lands?

Ourland	Lilliput	Dimutia	Quarterville	Micropolus	Small Town
100 inches					
75 inches					
50 inches					
25 inches					
10 inches					

Write a Guide for Using the Table

Explain how you can use your table to answer each question.

- If an object is 80 inches long in Ourland, how long would it be in each of the other lands?

- If an object is 5 inches long in Lilliput, how long would it be in Ourland?

- If an object is 25 inches long in Small Town, how long would it be in the other lands?

hot **words** | coordinate graph

Homework

page 317

GULLIVER'S WORLDS • LESSON 10 303

Rescaling in One, Two, and Three Dimensions

We were really short of materials in my classroom, so I used a combination of paper and 3-D manipulatives. I found that each group needed to work with the 3-D cubes on at least one scale to truly understand the concept of volume, or how cubes are needed to fill cubes. To that end, I rotated the manipulatives so that each group worked with the Linker Cubes and Centimeter Cubes at least once during the lesson. □

I had to remind some students to count the number of squares of the face that was resting on the desk. I asked those students to group their numbers by face and reminded them that there were six faces to a cube. This served as a convenient check for both of us. □

Gulliver's Worlds Cubed

1 Reviewing Area and Volume

To introduce notation for measurement units and review aspects of area and volume, have students answer the questions that follow and those on the comment card in small groups or in a class discussion. Encourage them to use the information on page 304 to help them explain why we use square and cubic units for area and volume. During the discussion, all students should come to understand that they need a measurement unit that has area to measure area and a measurement unit that has volume to measure volume.

- Why did Gulliver need more than 12 Lilliputian mattresses to make a bed?

- Could we measure length in square inches? Why or why not?

- Why don't we use square inches to measure volume?

As students verbally describe the measurement units for area and volume, emphasize that we write square units as cm^2 or $in.^2$ and cubic units as cm^3 or $in.^3$ You may want to connect the exponent to the number of dimensions described by the unit. For example, if two dimensions are described, then we need square units (cm^2) to describe the measurements.

2 Investigating Cube Sizes in Different Lands

student page

Have students form groups to complete the investigation. Depending on the resources in the classroom, students can use centimeter cubes, LinkerCubes®, or their own 3-D cubes made out of paper to represent the size of an Ourland cube. Have students work together to create cubes at each of the scales listed (2, 3, and 4) and record the number of Ourland cubes used to make each cube. Encourage groups to estimate how many cubes it would take to make a Brobdingnag cube and share their estimates with other groups ($12^3 = 1,728$).

This activity reinforces an idea that students explored in earlier lessons: the area and volume of a scaled-up object are multiplied by much more than the scale factor. Later in this lesson, students will describe the mathematical connections among scale, length, area, and volume.

An Answer Key for item 1 can be found on Assessment page A24.

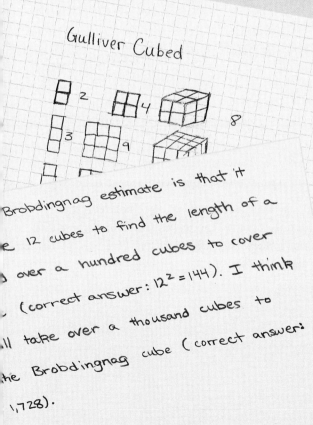

Gulliver Cubed

Brobdingnag estimate is that it
... 12 cubes to find the length of a
... over a hundred cubes to cover
... (correct answer: $12^2 = 144$). I think
... take over a thousand cubes to
... the Brobdingnag cube (correct answer:
$1,728$).

11 Gulliver's Worlds Cubed

RESCALING IN ONE,
TWO, AND THREE
DIMENSIONS

The *Gulliver's Worlds* group exhibit needs a finishing touch. The exhibit needs to show how rescaling affects area and volume. How do length, area, and volume change when the scale of something changes? Can you create a display that will help visitors understand this?

Investigate Cube Sizes in Different Lands

How does a change in scale affect measurements of length, area, and volume?

Use the information on this page to figure out a way to use Ourland cubes to build a large cube at each of the following scale factors: 2:1, 3:1, 4:1.

1 Record how many Ourland cubes make up each large cube.

2 Estimate how many cubes it would take to make a Brobdingnag cube (scale factor = 12:1)

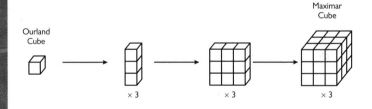

Ourland Cube

Maximar Cube

×3   ×3   ×3

Comment Card

If Maximar is 3 times bigger than Ourland, why does it take more than 3 cubes from Ourland to make a cube in Maximar?

304   **GULLIVER'S WORLDS** • LESSON 11

I challenged a few of my students by having them add some of the reducing scales (Lilliput, Dimutia) to their charts. Some students found that they were forced to rethink their rules, while others discovered new patterns. □

I wanted my students to use exponents to describe all the measurements on their charts—but I found that a few students had made cubes that were not a clear centimeter or inch cube. I let those students use nonstandard units to describe their measurements. Some referred back to the mum-gluffs of Lesson 6 and others made up their own unit (toto^2). This way, all my students were able to use the exponents successfully and still maintain the integrity of their cubes. □

3 Collecting Data for Two and Three Dimensions

student page

Students should begin the investigation by using their cubes from the previous step to answer each question and organize the answers into a table. You can also use the following questions as part of a class discussion to help students fill in the data for the Brobdingnag cube.

- How many Ourland cubes would it take to cover a face of the Brobdingnag cube? to fill the Brobdingnag cube? Why is this true, if the scale is 1:12?

- How would you describe the area of a face of the Brobdingnag cube? What's the volume of this cube? Were you able to build one? Why or why not?

When students have finished the first four steps of the investigation, have them come up with a rule they can use to predict what would happen if they made a cube at each of the following scales: 6, 25, 100, and 2.5. Students should complete their tables using their rule for each scale. To help them discover rules, you can have them look for patterns in their table. To save time, this step may be assigned as homework.

> An Answer Key for items 1–2 can be found on Assessment page A24.

4 Writing About Scale, Area, and Volume

student page

As students present their tables and rules, use the following questions to help them see connections among scale, length, area, and volume. By the end of this discussion, they should understand that area increases as the square of the scale factor and that volume increases as the cube of the scale factor. Have students adjust their charts to include how the number of cubes translates into standard measurement units and exponents. Students should write down their rules and explain their reasoning using a diagram.

- What did you discover about how the side length, face area, and volume of a cube relate to the scale?

- How could you use exponents to describe your discoveries?

- How would you use exponents to write the area and volume of a cube with a scale of 5?

- What connection do you see between these exponents and the terms *two-dimensional* and *three-dimensional*?

DOES STUDENTS' WORK SHOW:

- *an ability to explain the relationship between rescaling and area and volume measurements?*
- *an ability to create a rule to predict changes in area and volume measurements?*
- *correct use of exponents with measurement units?*
- *understanding of the differences between linear, area, and volume measurement?*

See *Gulliver's Worlds* Assessment page A13 for assessment information.

Collect Data for Two and Three Dimensions

Use your cubes to collect size information.

1 Organize the information into a table that answers the following questions:

a. What is the scale factor of the cube?

b. How many Ourland cubes high is one edge of this cube?

c. How many Ourland cubes are needed to cover one face of this cube completely?

d. How many Ourland cubes are needed to fill this cube completely?

> **How can you predict how much each measurement will change when you rescale?**

Scale Factor	How Many Cubes Long Is an Edge? (length)	How Many Cubes Cover a Face? (area)	How Many Cubes Fill the Cube? (volume)
2:1			
3:1			
4:1			
5:1			
10:1			
25:1			

2 Find a rule that can predict how big a cube would be for each of the following scales. Then add the information to your table:

2.5:1   6:1   20:1   100:1

Write About Scale, Area, and Volume

Write down the set of rules you used to complete your table. Make sure that someone else could apply your rules to any scale factor.

1 Explain how your rules work.

2 Make a diagram showing how to use the rules to predict the following:

a. The length of one edge of a cube

b. The area of one face of a cube

c. The volume of a cube

hot **words** | exponent
cubic centimeter

H💡mework
page 318

Final Project

Some students were not that familiar with museums that were interactive. I pointed out that often children's museums or technology museums allowed you to touch things and play games to understand the different displays. I had students imagine how it would be different if they were allowed to climb up on the dinosaur display to understand just how big they were, or use a computer to figure out how many of their footprints would fit inside the footprint of a T-Rex. □

When I had my students do their final projects in groups, I found I had to be very careful that they documented what they had done. I asked them to sign their work and also to turn in individual museum guides that explained the process. □

Stepping into Gulliver's Worlds

1 Planning a Life-Size Display

Refer students to the newspaper article on page 306 of the Student Guide and point out that in this lesson they will use the class displays from Lessons 9–11 and their writing to create their own life-size display at the Ourland Museum.

As a class, brainstorm what could be included in a life-size display about a particular Land of the Large or a Land of the Little. It helps students to get started on the project if they first visualize what a display could look like in the classroom. You may want to set up class guidelines for the displays concerning size, number of objects, and use of classroom materials (cubes, computers, video, etc.). Remind students that visitors to the museum will be from Ourland and therefore will be the same size as Gulliver.

In the final project, students should demonstrate their learning from the entire unit by making drawings according to a scale factor, creating an object in one, two, or three dimensions, choosing the appropriate units to measure, and communicating about linear, area, and volume measurements using exponents and/or comparisons.

2 Creating a Display Using Accurate Dimensions

Students should create an interactive display that helps visitors to the museum feel what it would be like to actually step into one of Gulliver's Worlds. Encourage students to make themselves part of the display and present a short tour using charts and words that describe and compare the sizes of objects in the display. To save time, you may want to have students work in groups to research the measurements, write the presentation, and build the objects in the display.

The final project is intentionally open-ended. Depending on the needs and special talents of your students, the displays can incorporate the fine arts, technology, or be presented entirely in the form of an individual museum guide with illustrations. This project also works well as an interdisciplinary activity.

homework options

LESSON HOMEWORK
Page 319

Creating a Display in

Bigville

Name of Land you have chosen

By: _____

Scale factor to Ourland: 10 : 1

Follow these steps to plan your display:
1. Description of Objects in the Display: Create at least three objects in one, two or three dimensions that will be part of the display.

Object	Dimensions (1-D, 2-D, 3-D)	Measurements
fork	2D	
spoon	3D	68" x 5"
plate	2D	55" x 10" x 5"
		100" x 5"

resentation: Write a short presentation that describes the measurements of the objects in
display and compares them to Ourland. Describe and label the area and volume of the
cts.

y display will have a 3-D flower vase
a 2D fork and plate. We will
ow the sketches of we made them.

ctive: Write a short description of how the visitors to the museum can step into the
lay group will have a dinner party
lay with questions and a place where
e can pretend to eat.

Include your writing and any graphs or charts that will help museum visitors to
d Gulliver's Worlds.

re going to people guess how big
ate would be in different lands.
re using the Lands of the Large
graph (Lesson 10) to help
guess.

---

12 Stepping into Gulliver's Worlds

FINAL PROJECT

A life-size display in the correct scale and proportion can make you feel like you have stepped into another world. You will help the Ourland Museum create a life-size display of one of the lands in *Gulliver's Worlds*. The goal is for museum visitors to get involved with your display.

What would it look like if you stepped into one of the lands in *Gulliver's Worlds*?

Create a Display Using Accurate Dimensions

Choose one of the lands in *Gulliver's Worlds*. Create a display and tour that compares the sizes of things in that land to those in Ourland.

1 Create at least three objects in one, two, or three dimensions to use in the display.

2 Write a short tour that describes the measurements of the objects in the display and compares them to sizes in Ourland. Describe and label the areas and volumes of the objects.

3 Find a way for visitors to get involved with the display.

4 Include your writing from previous lessons and charts to help museum visitors understand the scale of the land.

Gulliver Show Opens At The Ourland Living Museum

by Jonathan Swift
Ourland News Correspondent

The Gulliver's Worlds exhibit at the Ourland Living Museum is an exciting journey to new lands. From my entrance, where I was met by a huge smile from a life-size Brobdingnag face, to the carefully crafted scale drawings of the Lands of the Little gallery, the exhibit showed this reporter what it would be like to actually live in the worlds that Gulliver explored hundreds of years ago in his famous journal.

306   GULLIVER'S WORLDS • LESSON 12

In one class, I had my students work in groups to observe all of the displays, and in my other class, I assigned specific displays to individual observers. I found that both systems worked equally well. I evaluated each display along with my students, using the task-specific rubric in the assessment pages (A15). ☐

I worked with my interdisciplinary team to present a 2-hour Gulliver's Worlds museum as part of a back-to-school night. I decided to have students present in 30-minute shifts, so that they could tour each other's displays. It also helped me and my colleagues have the time to observe all the displays (there are 120 students in my team). At the end of the unit, when students turned in their projects with the reviews and self-evaluations, I was able to evaluate each student individually using lots of different resources. ☐

3 Observing a Display

As the displays are presented, students should write down their observations for at least one display. To make sure each display is observed by at least one person, you may want to assign specific displays to specific students. Remind students to carefully note the scale factor of the display they are observing and identify the objects in the display they want to check in the next step.

To present their final projects, students can transform the classroom or the library into an Ourland Museum that is open to parents and other students. Each group or individual should make several presentations as visitors tour the display. The museum could also include displays from Lessons 9–11 as well as students' individual writing. You may want to distribute the Comment Card, Reproducible R23, to help visitors to the museum give feedback to the student presenters.

4 Reviewing a Display

student page

After all the displays have been presented, have students come up with a way to quickly check whether or not the objects in a display are the correct scale. Have them write reviews that can be given to the creator(s) of the display. The reviews should include accurate information about the length, area, and volume measurements of the objects in the display, and about how the observers checked those measurements.

Students may use cubes, graph paper, string, or any other device to check the sizes of things found in the display. Encourage students who are still using nonstandard measurement tools (string, fingers) to compare sizes to describe their measurements in standard units as well.

5 Evaluating the Gulliver's Worlds Exhibit

When students receive the reviews for their displays, you may want to have them self-evaluate using the Student Assessment Criteria, Reproducible R6. Students can also reflect on their learning from the entire unit using the Post-assessment, page A17, as a writing prompt.

Review a Display

You will be reviewing a classmate's display and presentation. As you review the exhibit, write down the scale factor and as many measurements as you can. Use the following questions to help write your review:

1 What parts of the display look life-size?

2 How did you check that the sizes of the objects in the display were correct?

3 How does the presentation describe linear, area, and volume measurements?

4 How does the presentation compare sizes to those in Ourland?

5 Would you add or change anything to make the display more believable?

How would you evaluate your own display?

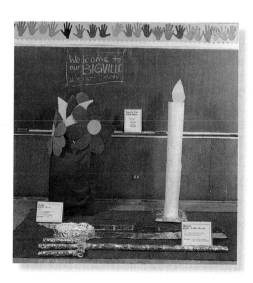

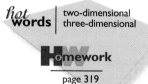

hot **words** | two-dimensional three-dimensional

Ho**mework**
page 319

The Sizes of Things in Brobdingnag

Applying Skills

Fill in the missing height conversions to complete the chart.

	Name	Height (in.)	Height (ft and in.)	Height (ft)
	Marla	49″	4′1″	$4\frac{1}{12}′$
1.	Scott	56″		
2.	Jessica		4′7″	
3.	Shoshana	63″		
4.	Jamal	54″		
5.	Louise		4′11″	
6.	Kelvin	58″		
7.	Keisha		5′2″	
8.	Jeffrey		4′2″	

9. List the names in height order from tallest to shortest.

10. The scale factor of Giantland to Ourland is 11:1. That means that objects in Giantland are 11 times the size of the same objects in Ourland. Figure out how large the following Ourland objects would be in Giantland:

a. a tree that is 9 ft tall

b. a man that is 6 ft tall

c. a photo that is 7 in. wide and 5 in. high

11. The scale factor of Big City to Ourland is 5:1. That means that objects in Big City are 5 times the size of the same objects in Ourland. How large would each of the Ourland objects from item **10** be in Big City?

Extending Concepts

12. Duane made an amazing run at the football game Friday night.

Examine the diagram below and give the distance of the play in:

a. yards   **b.** feet   **c.** inches

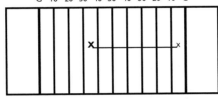

HINT: From goal line to goal line in a football field is 100 yards.

Making Connections

13. Answer this Dr. Math letter:

Dear Dr. Math,

Today in science class we were using microscopes. The lenses were 10×, 50×, and 100×. I think there is a way scale factor applies to what I see and what the actual size is. Is that true? If so, could you please explain?

William Neye

Homework

Solutions: Lesson 1

	Name	Height (in.)	Height (ft and in.)	Height (ft)
1.	Scott	56″	4′ 8″	$4\frac{2}{3}′$
2.	Jessica	55″	4′ 7″	$4\frac{7}{12}′$
3.	Shoshana	63″	5′ 3″	$5\frac{1}{4}′$
4.	Jamal	54″	4′ 6″	$4\frac{1}{2}′$
5.	Louise	59″	4′ 11″	$4\frac{11}{12}′$
6.	Kelvin	58″	4′ 10″	$4\frac{5}{6}′$
7.	Keisha	62″	5′ 2″	$5\frac{1}{6}′$
8.	Jeffrey	50″	4′ 2″	$4\frac{1}{6}′$

9. Shoshana, Keisha, Louise, Kelvin, Scott, Jessica, Jamal, Jeffrey, Marla

10. a. 99 ft

b. 66 ft

c. 77 in. × 55 in.

11. a. 45 ft

b. 30 ft

c. 35 in. × 25 in.

12. a. 60 yd

b. 180 ft

c. 2,160 in.

13. Yes. The 10× lens results in a scale of 10:1. The item on the microscope slide is the 1, and what you see when you look in the eyepiece is 10 times larger. Likewise 50× is 50:1, and 100× is 100:1.

Solutions: Lesson 2

1. $\frac{3}{7}$

2. $\frac{11}{42}$

3. $\frac{2}{3}$

4. $\frac{7}{12}$

5. $\frac{1}{5}$

6. $\frac{5}{9}$

7. $\frac{1}{2}$

8. $\frac{1}{3}$

9. $1\frac{1}{3}$

10. $10\frac{2}{3}$

11. 10:1

12. $\frac{4}{1}$

13. $\frac{2}{1}$

14. six to one

15. 8:1

16. 14:1

17. **a.** 90 ft high × 160 ft long
    b. 460 yd high × 800 ft long
    c. 170 in. × 220 in.

18. **a.** 120:1
    b. 1 ft 3 in.

A Life-Size Object in Brobdingnag

Applying Skills

Reduce these fractions to lowest terms.

1. $\frac{21}{49}$ 2. $\frac{33}{126}$ 3. $\frac{54}{81}$

4. $\frac{28}{48}$ 5. $\frac{15}{75}$ 6. $\frac{10}{18}$

7. $\frac{126}{252}$ 8. $\frac{8}{24}$ 9. $\frac{16}{12}$

10. $\frac{64}{6}$

Follow the instructions to describe each relationship in a different way.

11. Write $\frac{10}{1}$ as a ratio.

12. Write 4:1 as a fraction.

13. Write "2 to 1" as a fraction.

14. Write out 6:1 in words.

15. Write $\frac{8}{1}$ as a ratio.

Extending Concepts

16. The height of a blade of grass in a giant-size display is $4\frac{2}{3}$ ft. The blade of grass in your yard is 4 in. high. What is the scale factor?

$4\frac{2}{3}$ ft

17. The scale factor of Vastland to Ourland is 20:1. That means that objects in Vastland are 20 times the size of the same objects in Ourland. Figure out how large the following Ourland objects would be in Vastland:

    a. a car that is $4\frac{1}{2}$ ft high and 8 ft long

    b. a building that is 23 yd high and 40 ft long

    c. a piece of paper that is $8\frac{1}{2}$ in. wide and 11 in. long

Making Connections

18. The science class is creating insects that are larger than life. First they will study the ant. The queen ant that they have to observe is $\frac{1}{2}$ in. long. The large model they create will be 5 ft long. Mr. Estes wants to have a ladybug model created too. Tasha found a ladybug and measured it at $\frac{1}{8}$ in. long.

$\frac{1}{2}$ in.

    a. What is the scale factor for the ant model?

    b. How big will the ladybug model be if the same scale factor is used?

How Big Is "Little" Glumdalclitch?

Applying Skills

Reduce these fractions to the lowest terms.

1. $\frac{25}{75}$ **2.** $\frac{69}{23}$ **3.** $\frac{1,176}{21}$

4. $\frac{16}{4}$ **5.** $\frac{36}{30}$ **6.** $\frac{49}{14}$

7. $\frac{24}{3}$ **8.** $\frac{54}{18}$ **9.** $\frac{8}{12}$

Convert these fractions to like measurement units and then reduce each fraction to show a size relationship. See if you can make each fraction into a scale factor.

10. $\frac{3 \text{ in.}}{4 \text{ ft}}$ **11.** $\frac{8 \text{ in.}}{2 \text{ yd}}$ **12.** $\frac{440 \text{ yd}}{\frac{1}{2} \text{ mi}}$

13. $\frac{18 \text{ in.}}{1 \text{ yd}}$ **14.** $\frac{2 \text{ yd}}{12 \text{ ft}}$

Extending Concepts

15. Ali is writing a script for a new movie in which aliens that are 3 times the size of humans (3:1) take the game of football back to their home planet. HINT: U.S. regulation football fields measure 100 yards from goal line to goal line.

a. How long is the aliens' field in yards?

b. How long is the aliens' field in inches?

c. How long is the aliens' field in feet?

16. The scale factor of Jumbolia to Ourland is 17:1. That means that objects in Jumbolia are 17 times the size of the same objects in Ourland. Figure out how large the following Ourland objects would be in Jumbolia:

a. a radio that is $4\frac{1}{2}$ in. high, 8 in. long, and $3\frac{1}{2}$ in. wide

b. a rug that is $6\frac{1}{2}$ ft wide and $9\frac{3}{4}$ ft long

c. a desk that is $2\frac{1}{3}$ ft high, 3 ft long, and $2\frac{1}{2}$ ft wide

Making Connections

17. Provide the scale factor for the following map by measuring the distance with a ruler. The distance from the library to the school is $2\frac{1}{2}$ miles.

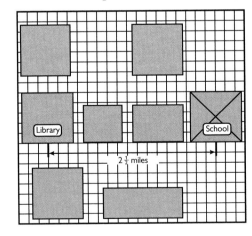

Homework

Solutions: Lesson 3

1. $\frac{1}{3}$

2. 3

3. 56

4. 4

5. $1\frac{1}{5}$

6. $3\frac{1}{2}$

7. 8

8. 3

9. $\frac{2}{3}$

10. $\frac{3 \text{ in.}}{48 \text{ in.}}$; $\frac{1}{16}$

11. $\frac{8 \text{ in.}}{72 \text{in.}}$; $\frac{1}{9}$

12. $\frac{440 \text{ yd}}{880 \text{ yd}}$; $\frac{1}{2}$

13. $\frac{18 \text{ in.}}{36 \text{ in.}}$; $\frac{1}{2}$

14. $\frac{6 \text{ ft}}{12 \text{ ft}}$; $\frac{1}{2}$

15. a. 300 yds
    b. 10,800 in.
    c. 900 ft

16. a. $76\frac{1}{2}$ in. $\times$ 136 in. $\times$ $59\frac{1}{2}$ in.

    b. $110\frac{1}{2}$ ft $\times$ $165\frac{3}{4}$ ft

    c. $39\frac{2}{3}$ ft $\times$ 51 ft $\times$ $42\frac{1}{2}$ ft

17. The scale factor is 1 in:1 mi. or 1:63,360

Solutions: Lesson 4

1. $\frac{9 \text{ in.}}{3 \text{ in.}}$; 3:1

2. $\frac{6 \text{ ft}}{1 \text{ ft}}$; 6:1

3. $\frac{2,640 \text{ ft}}{528 \text{ ft}}$; 5:1

4. $\frac{90 \text{ in.}}{3 \text{ in.}}$; 30:1

5. $\frac{14 \text{ in.}}{7 \text{ in.}}$; 2:1

6. $\frac{6 \text{ in.}}{2 \text{ in.}}$; 3:1

7. $\frac{352 \text{ ft}}{16 \text{ ft}}$; 22:1

8. $\frac{49 \text{ in.}}{7 \text{ in.}}$; 7:1

9. $\frac{4 \text{ mi}}{1 \text{ mi}}$; 4:1

10. $\frac{366 \text{ ft}}{6 \text{ ft}}$; 61:1

11. **a.** 5 yd tall × $2\frac{1}{2}$ yd wide

    b. 3,600 yd

    c. 126 ft high × 144 ft wide × 72 yd long

12. scale factor 3:1

    a. 15 in. tall × $7\frac{1}{2}$ in. wide

    b. 300 yd

    c. $10\frac{1}{2}$ ft high × 12 ft wide × 6 yd long

13. **a. iii.** (3:1 = 1 yd : 1 ft)

    b. iv. (5,280:1 = 1 mi:1 ft)

    c. i. (12:1 = 1 ft:1 in.)

    d. ii. (1,760:1 = 1 mi:1 yd)

14. Size of postage stamp: 4 in. × 6 in.

Telling Tales in Brobdingnag

Applying Skills

Convert these ratios to like measurement units and then reduce the fraction to create a scale factor.

Example $\frac{1}{2}$ yd: 6 in. $= \frac{\frac{1}{2}\text{ yd}}{6 \text{ in.}} = \frac{18 \text{ in.}}{6 \text{ in.}} = \frac{3 \text{ in.}}{1 \text{ in.}} =$ scale factor 3:1

1. $\frac{3}{4}$ ft:3 in.

2. 6 ft: $\frac{1}{3}$ yd

3. $\frac{1}{2}$ mi : 528 ft

4. $2\frac{1}{2}$ yd: $\frac{1}{4}$ ft

5. 14 in : $\frac{7}{12}$ ft

6. $\frac{1}{6}$ yd:2 in.

7. $\frac{1}{15}$ mi:16 ft

8. $4\frac{1}{12}$ ft:7 in.

9. 4 mi:1,760 yd

10. 4,392 in:6 ft

Extending Concepts

11. The scale factor of Mammothville to Ourland is 1 yd:1 in. That means if an object in Mammothville is one yard long, then the same object in Ourland would be only one inch long. Figure out how large the following Ourland objects would be in Mammothville:

    a. a soda can that is 5 in. tall and $2\frac{1}{2}$ in. wide

    b. a football field that is 100 yd long

    c. a table that is $3\frac{1}{2}$ ft high, 4 ft wide, and 2 yd long

12. The scale factor of Colossus to Ourland is $\frac{1}{4}$ yd:3 in. That means if an object in Colossus is $\frac{1}{4}$ of a yard long, then the same object in Ourland would be only 3 inches long. How large would each of the Ourland objects from item **11** be in Colossus?

13. Match the following scale factors to the correct measurement units:

    a. 3:1   **i.** 1 ft:1 in.

    b. 5,280:1   **ii.** 1 mi:1 yd

    c. 12:1   **iii.** 1 yd:1 ft

    d. 1,760:1   **iv.** 1 mi:1 ft

Making Connections

14. In Humungoville the scale factor to Ourland is 4:1. Use the postage stamp from Ourland pictured below to draw a postage stamp for Humungoville. Make sure the length and width are at a scale factor of 4:1. You can be creative with the picture inside.

Sizing Up the Lilliputians

Applying Skills

Write each of the following decimals as a fraction.

Example $0.302 = \dfrac{302}{1,000}$

1. 0.2 **2.** 0.435

3. 0.1056 **4.** 0.78

5. 0.44 **6.** 0.025

7. 0.9 **8.** 0.5002

9. 0.001 **10.** 0.67

Write each decimal in words.

Example 0.5 = five tenths

11. 0.007 **12.** 0.25

13. 0.3892 **14.** 0.6

15. 0.04

16. The scale factor of Pint-Size Place to Ourland is 1:11. That means that objects in Ourland are 11 times the size of the same objects in Pint-Size Place. Figure out about how large the following Ourland objects would be in Pint-Size Place:

   a. a house that is 15 ft high, 33 ft wide, and 60 ft long

   b. a train that is 363 ft long and 20 ft high

   c. a woman who is 5 ft 6 in. tall

Extending Concepts

17. Measure the height of each picture. Compare the sizes of the pictures and determine the scale factor. What is the scale factor when:

   a. the larger picture is 1?

   b. the smaller picture is 1?

Making Connections

18. The regulation size of a soccer field varies from the largest size, 119 m × 91 m, to the smallest size allowed, 91 m × 46 m. What is the difference in the perimeters of the two field sizes? How do you think the difference in perimeters affects the game?

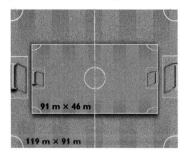

91 m × 46 m

119 m × 91 m

Homework

Solutions: Lesson 5

1. $\dfrac{2}{10}$

2. $\dfrac{435}{1,000}$

3. $\dfrac{1,056}{10,000}$

4. $\dfrac{78}{100}$

5. $\dfrac{44}{100}$

6. $\dfrac{25}{1,000}$

7. $\dfrac{9}{10}$

8. $\dfrac{5,002}{10,000}$

9. $\dfrac{1}{1,000}$

10. $\dfrac{67}{100}$

11. seven thousandths

12. twenty-five hundredths

13. three thousand eight hundred ninety-two ten-thousandths

14. six tenths

15. four one-hundredths

16. **a.** $1\frac{1}{3}$ ft high × 3 ft wide × $5\frac{1}{2}$ ft long

    b. 33 ft long × 22 in. high

    c. 6 in. tall

17. **a.** 0.5:1

    b. 1:2

18. 146 m

Solutions: Lesson 6

	mm	cm	dm	m	km
1.	1,000,000	100,000	10,000	1,000	1
2.	1,000	100	10	1	0.001
3.	100	10	1	0.1	0.0001
4.	10	1	0.1	0.01	0.00001
5.	1	0.1	0.01	0.001	0.000001

6. 4.2 m

7. 0.05 m

8. 50 cm

9. 2.5 mm

10. 450 m

11. 12.7 dm

12. 245 cm

13. 0.3869 m

14. 0.02 cm

15. 369.782 m

16. 1.28 mm

17. 73 dm

18. 43.5 cm, 0.5 m, 7 dm, 1,967 mm, 0.0073 km

19. a. 12 units; 9 square units

    b. 24 units; 36 square units

20. Perimeters: 1:2

    Areas: 1:4

Glum-gluffs and Mum-gluffs

Applying Skills

Complete the following table showing equivalencies in the metric system.

	mm	cm	dm	m	km
1.				1,000	1
2.	1,000	100	10	1	
3.			1		
4.		1			
5.	1				

Supply the missing equivalent.

6. 42 dm = _____ m

7. 5 cm = _____ m

8. 0.5 m = _____ cm

9. 0.25 cm = _____ mm

10. 0.45 km = _____ m

11. 1.27 m = _____ dm

12. 24.5 dm = _____ cm

13. 38.69 cm = _____ m

14. 0.2 mm = _____ cm

15. 369,782 mm = _____ m

16. 0.128 cm = _____ mm

17. 7.3 m = _____ dm

Extending Concepts

18. Place the following measurements in height order from shortest to tallest.

- 1967 mm
- 0.0073 km
- 43.5 cm
- 0.5 m
- 7 dm

Making Connections

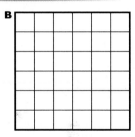

19. Count the smaller squares to figure out the sizes of squares A and B in square units.

    a. What are the perimeter and the area of square A?

    b. What are the perimeter and the area of square B?

20. Compare the two perimeters and the two areas. Describe each size relationship using a scale factor.

Housing and Feeding Gulliver

Applying Skills

Convert these fractions to like measurement units.

Example $\dfrac{4 \text{ m}}{4 \text{ cm}} = \dfrac{400 \text{ cm}}{4 \text{ cm}}$

1. $\dfrac{43 \text{ cm}}{43 \text{ mm}}$ **2.** $\dfrac{5 \text{ m}}{5 \text{ cm}}$ **3.** $\dfrac{6 \text{ km}}{6 \text{ m}}$

Use your answers from items 1–3 to show a scale factor that is less than one.
HINT: Reduce the larger number to one.

Example $\dfrac{400 \text{ cm} \div 400}{4 \text{ cm} \div 400} = \dfrac{1}{0.01} = 1{:}0.01$

4. $\dfrac{43 \text{ cm}}{43 \text{ mm}}$ **5.** $\dfrac{5 \text{ m}}{5 \text{ cm}}$ **6.** $\dfrac{6 \text{ km}}{6 \text{ m}}$

7. The scale factor of Teeny Town to Ourland is 1:6. That means that objects in Ourland are 6 times the size of the same objects in Teeny Town. Figure out how large the following Ourland objects would be in Teeny Town:

a. a book 30 cm high and 24 cm wide

b. a girl 156 cm tall

c. a table 1 m high, 150 cm wide, and 2 m long

Extending Concepts

8. Albert is using a scale factor of 3:1 for his school project. The height of the walls he measured are 3 m and the walls in the model he made are 1 m high. A 3-ft-high chair became a 1-ft-high chair in his project. Can he use both metric and U.S. customary measurement units in the same project? Why or why not?

9. The scale factor of Itty-Bittyville to Ourland is 1:4. That means that objects in Ourland are 4 times the size of the same objects in Itty-Bittyville. Estimate the sizes of each of the following Itty-Bittyville objects and find an object in Ourland that is about the same size:

a. an Itty-Bittyville textbook

b. an Itty-Bittyville double bed

c. an Itty-Bittyville two-story building

d. an Itty-Bittyville car

10. Estimate the scale factor of Peeweeopolis to Ourland if the area of an Ourland postage stamp is equal to the area of a Peeweeopolis sheet of paper.

Making Connections

For items 11–13 use the figure below.

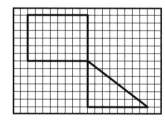

11. What is the area in square units of:

    a. the rectangle?   **b.** the triangle?

12. Enlarge each shape using a scale factor of 3:1. What is the area in square units of:

    a. the rectangle?   **b.** the triangle?

13. How did you figure out the area of each shape for items 11 and 12?

Homework

Solutions: Lesson 7

1. $\dfrac{430 \text{ mm}}{43 \text{ mm}}$

2. $\dfrac{500 \text{ cm}}{5 \text{ cm}}$

3. $\dfrac{6{,}000 \text{ m}}{6 \text{ m}}$

4. 1:0.1

5. 1:0.01

6. 1:0.001

7. **a.** 5 cm high × 4 cm wide
   b. 26 cm
   c. $16\frac{2}{3}$ cm high × 25 cm wide × $33\frac{1}{3}$ cm long

8. Yes. He can use any measurement system as long as he keeps the scale at 3:1.

9. Answers will vary.

10. Answers will vary. Possible answer: 1:11

11. **a.** 48 square units   **b.** 24 square units

12. **a.** 432 square units   **b.** 216 square units

13. Multiply each area by 3 × 3 or 9.

Solutions: Lesson 8

1. $1\frac{2}{7}$

2. $\frac{1}{6}$

3. $\frac{4}{5}$

4. $\frac{1}{10}$

5. $\frac{3}{4}$

6. $\frac{3}{4}$

7. $\frac{3}{4}$

8. $1\frac{1}{5}$

9. $\frac{3}{4}$

10. $\frac{1}{3}$

11. $\frac{2}{3}$

12. $3\frac{1}{5}$

13. $\frac{1}{2}$

14. $\frac{1}{3}$

15. **a.** U.S. customary
    b. metric

16. **a.** 21 ft high × 11 ft wide × 12 ft long
    b. approximately $1{,}508\frac{1}{2}$ ft
    c. approximately 1 in. × $1\frac{1}{2}$ in.

17. **a.** 2 cm:1 ft
    b. 86 ft wide, 30 ft long

Seeing Through Lilliputian Eyes

Applying Skills

Reduce the following fractions to the lowest terms.

Example $\dfrac{36}{42} = \dfrac{6}{7}$

1. $\dfrac{81}{63}$ 2. $\dfrac{4}{24}$ 3. $\dfrac{16}{20}$

4. $\dfrac{5}{50}$ 5. $\dfrac{27}{36}$ 6. $\dfrac{36}{48}$

7. $\dfrac{90}{120}$ 8. $\dfrac{12}{10}$ 9. $\dfrac{75}{100}$

10. $\dfrac{11}{33}$ 11. $\dfrac{14}{21}$ 12. $\dfrac{80}{25}$

13. $\dfrac{9}{18}$ 14. $\dfrac{4}{12}$

Making Connections

17. In science-fiction movies, miniatures and scale-factor models are used to create many of the special effects. In one case, the special effects team created several different scale models of the hero's spaceship. The life-size ship that was built to use for the filming was 60 ft long. One scale model was 122 cm long by 173 cm wide by 61 cm high.

    a. What was the scale factor?

    b. What were the width and height of the life-size ship?

Extending Concepts

15. Measure the length and width of each of the following shapes. Which measurement system, metric or U.S. customary, would be the easiest to use to enlarge each object using a scale factor of 2:1? Why?

    a.   **b.**

16. The scale factor of Miniopolis to Ourland is 1:7. That means that objects in Miniopolis are $\frac{1}{7}$ the size of the same objects in Ourland. Figure out how large the following Ourland objects would be in Miniopolis:

    a. a building that is 147 ft high, 77 ft wide, and 84 ft long

    b. a road that is 2 miles long

    c. a piece of paper that is $8\frac{1}{2}$ in. by 11 in.

Lands of the Large

Applying Skills

In the following exercises provide equivalent decimals.

Example $\frac{1}{2} = 0.5$

1. $\frac{1}{20}$ **2.** $\frac{1}{3}$ **3.** $\frac{1}{4}$

4. $\frac{1}{5}$ **5.** $\frac{1}{10}$ **6.** $\frac{1}{8}$

7. $\frac{3}{4}$ **8.** $\frac{1}{7}$

9. The scale factor of Big City to Ourland is 6.5:1. That means that objects in Big City are 6.5 times the size of the same objects in Ourland. Figure out how large the following Ourland objects would be in Big City:

a. a tree that is 9 ft tall

b. a man that is 6 ft tall

c. a photo that is 7 in. wide and 5 in. long

Extending Concepts

10. Complete the following table by figuring out equivalent scale factors for each row.

	Decimals	Fractions	Whole Numbers
	1.5:1	$1\frac{1}{2}$:1	3:2
a.	6.5:1		
b.		$8\frac{1}{4}$:1	
c.			5:3

11. The scale factor of Big City to Hugeville is 3:2. That means that objects in Big City are 1.5, or $1\frac{1}{2}$, times the size of the same objects in Hugeville. How large would each of the Big City objects from item **9** be in Hugeville?

Making Connections

12. The scale factor is 5:1 for a giant ice cube in comparison to the school cafeteria's ice cubes.

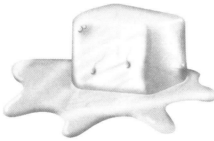

a. Draw a picture that shows how many cafeteria ice cubes you would have to stack high, wide, and deep to build a giant ice cube.

b. What is the total number of cafeteria ice cubes it would take to fill one giant ice cube?

Homework

Solutions: Lesson 9

1. 0.05

2. 0.$\bar{3}$

3. 0.25

4. 0.2

5. 0.1

6. 0.125

7. 0.75

8. approximately 0.143

9. a. $58\frac{1}{2}$ ft

 b. 39 ft

 c. $45\frac{1}{2}$ in. × $32\frac{1}{2}$ in.

10.

	Decimals	Fractions	Whole Numbers
a.	6.5:1	$6\frac{1}{2}$:1	13:2
b.	8.25:1	$8\frac{1}{4}$:1	33:4
c.	1.67:1	$1\frac{2}{3}$:1	5:3

11. scale factor is 1:$\frac{2}{3}$

 a. 39 ft

 b. 26 ft

 c. $30\frac{1}{3}$ in. × $21\frac{2}{3}$ in.

12. a.

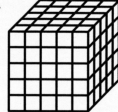

 b. 125 ice cubes

Solutions: Lesson 10

1. 0.5

2. $\frac{1}{4}$

3. $0.\bar{6}$

4. $\frac{7}{10}$

5. 0.75

6. $\frac{1}{20}$

7. 0.375

8. $\frac{1}{8}$

9. $\frac{3}{3}:\frac{2}{3}=1:\frac{2}{3}$

10. $\frac{4}{4}:\frac{3}{4}=1:\frac{3}{4}$

11. $\frac{5}{5}:\frac{3}{5}=1:\frac{3}{5}$

12. 0.1:1

13. 1:2

14. a. $7\frac{1}{2}$ ft high × $17\frac{1}{2}$ ft wide × 30 ft long

    b. 180 ft long × 10 ft high

    c. 2 ft 8 in.

15. It is the reciprocal; Yes.

Lands of the Little

Homework 10

Applying Skills

Complete the following chart by supplying the missing equivalents as decimals or fractions.

	Fractions	Decimals
1.	$\frac{1}{2}$	
2.		0.25
3.	$\frac{2}{3}$	
4.		0.7
5.	$\frac{3}{4}$	
6.		0.05
7.	$\frac{3}{8}$	
8.		0.125

Reduce the scale factor to a fraction. HINT: Divide each number by the largest number.

Example $10:7 = \frac{10}{10}:\frac{7}{10} = 1:\frac{7}{10}$

9. 3:2   10. 4:3   11. 5:3

Extending Concepts

12. The scale factor for Giantland to Ourland is 10:1. What is the scale factor from Ourland to Giantland? Write the scale factor using a decimal or fraction for Ourland to Giantland.

13. The scale factor of Wee World to Ourland is 0.5:1. That means that objects in Wee World are 0.5 the size of the same objects in Ourland. What is another way to write this scale factor without using a decimal?

14. Using the scale factor from item **13**, figure out how large the following Ourland objects would be in Wee World:

    a. a house that is 15 ft high, 35 ft wide, and 60 ft long

    b. a train that is 360 ft long and 20 ft high

    c. a woman who is 5 ft 4 in. tall

Making Connections

15. Answer this Dr. Math letter:

Dr. Math,

When I was doing problems 9–11 in today's homework, my friend said there was a pattern between the whole-number scale factor and the fraction scale factor. I don't see it. Can you please explain it to me? Could I use this pattern to rescale objects more efficiently?

D.S. Mall

Gulliver's Worlds Cubed

Applying Skills

Complete the following chart with equivalent expressions.

Exponent	Arithmetic Expression	Value
3^3	$3 \times 3 \times 3$	27
1. 2^2		
2.	$4 \times 4 \times 4$	
3.		25
4. 6^2		
5.		49
6. 8^3		
7.		81
8. 10^2		
9. 5^3		
10.	$6 \times 6 \times 6$	

Tell whether each unit of measurement would be used for area or volume.

11. yd^2 (square yard)

12. cm^3 (cubic centimeter)

13. m^2 (square meter)

14. in^2 (square inch)

15. ft^3 (cubic feet)

16. mm^3 (cubic millimeter)

Extending Concepts

17. Concrete To Go is going to pour a patio 4 yd long, 4 yd wide, and $\frac{1}{12}$ yd deep. Do they need to know the area or the volume to know how much concrete is needed? Come up with a strategy to figure out how much concrete they should pour.

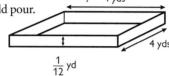

4 yds

4 yds

$\frac{1}{12}$ yd

Making Connections

18. Imagine you have been hired by a famous clothing designer. It is your job to purchase the fabric for the upcoming designs. Your boss asks you to draw a smaller version of the designer's most successful scarf using a scale factor of 1:3. The original scarf is one yard long and one yard wide.

a. Draw a pattern with measurements for the new smaller scarf.

b. The company will make one hundred smaller scarves using your new pattern. How much fabric should you purchase?

Solutions: Lesson 11

1. $2^2 = 2 \times 2 = 4$
2. $4^3 = 4 \times 4 \times 4 = 64$
3. $5^2 = 5 \times 5 = 25$
4. $6^2 = 6 \times 6 = 36$
5. $7^2 = 7 \times 7 = 49$
6. $8^3 = 8 \times 8 \times 8 = 512$
7. $9^2 = 9 \times 9 = 81$
8. $10^2 = 10 \times 10 = 100$
9. $5^3 = 5 \times 5 \times 5 = 125$
10. $6^3 = 6 \times 6 \times 6 = 216$
11. Area
12. Volume
13. Area
14. Area
15. Volume
16. Volume
17. Volume $(4 \times 4 \times \frac{1}{12} = 1\frac{1}{3} \text{ yd}^3)$
18. **a.** Drawing should measure 1 ft $\times$ 1 ft.
    b. 100 ft^2

Solutions: Lesson 12

1. $\frac{1}{8}$

2. 0.375

3. $\frac{3}{4}$

4. $\frac{2}{3}$

5. 0.5

6. $\frac{1}{5}$

7. 0.1

8. 0.05

9. a. $1 + 1 + 1 + 1 = 4$ in.

 b. $1 \times 1 = 1$ in.^{2}

10. $h = 2.5$ cm, $w = 2.5$ cm, $l = 2.5$ cm

11. a. cube with h, w, l, each labeled

 b. 1 ft^2

 c. 6 ft^2

12. a. 9 ft

 b. 24 in. × 60 in.

 c. 3 ft × 3 ft × 6 ft

Stepping into Gulliver's Worlds

Applying Skills

Complete the following chart by supplying the missing equivalents as decimals or fractions.

	Decimal	Fraction
1.	0.125	
2.		$\frac{3}{8}$
3.	0.75	
4.	0.67	
5.		$\frac{1}{2}$
6.	0.2	
7.		$\frac{1}{10}$
8.		$\frac{1}{20}$

9. Measure the sides of the square in inches. What is the:

a. perimeter?   **b.** area?

10. Use the metric system to measure the height, width, and length of the cube below.

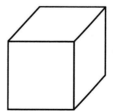

Extending Concepts

11. Shelley wants to cover a box with contact paper. The box is 1 ft high, 1 ft wide, and 1 ft deep.

 a. Draw the box and show the measurements.

 b. How many square feet of paper will she need to cover one face of the box?

 c. How many square feet will she need to cover all sides of the box?

Making Connections

12. The creator of a famous theme park wanted children to feel bigger than life. The scale factor of objects in real life to objects in the park is 1:0.75.

 a. Height of a street light?

 Real life: 12 ft

 Theme park:

 12 feet

 b. Length and width of a door?

 Real life: 32″ × 80″

 Theme park:

 c. Height, width, and depth of a box?

 Real life: 4 ft × 4 ft × 8 ft

 Theme park:

Assessment Overview

Many opportunities are provided in *Gulliver's Worlds* to assess student's conceptual understanding and skills related to scale and proportion, measurement, estimation, and data collection. This unit contains embedded end-of-phase assessments in Lessons 4, 8, and 12, the last serving as the unit assessment.

To start the unit, have students complete the pre-assessment activity on Teacher's Guide page 277E. Use this to assess readiness and growth throughout the unit when compared to students' work in Lesson 12. Also, you will find one skill quiz per phase on Reproducibles pages R2–R4. Guidance for optional portfolios is on pages A18–A19.

The *MathScape* assessment system provides flexibility and support for educators in a variety of situations. The core system uses three assessment tools to help you gather information, allowing you to monitor students' individual growth throughout the unit and evaluate their knowledge and abilities at the unit end. Notes from the classroom come from teachers who share their observations about student work, work evaluation, and ways to involve students in the assessment process. Teachers who have adapted the system have found it easy to meet their students' needs.

ASSESSMENT PHILOSOPHY

- Assessment is the shared responsibility of all who are concerned with students' learning in mathematics.

- An assessor can be a teacher, peer, or student.

- Assessment activities focus on what students do know and can do as opposed to what they don't know.

- Assessment activities don't use time as a factor, since speed is almost never relevant to mathematical effectiveness.

- An assessment tool can range from a skill quiz to an embedded, hands-on project.

- It takes a multifaceted assessment system combining traditional tests with performance assessment to create a complete picture of students' learning.

ASSESSMENT TOOLS

The three assessment tools—**What To Look For, Assessment Rubric,** and **Skill Check**—provide information for fully evaluating your students' learning. The information at the left shows where in the unit you can use each type of tool and on which Assessment page it is described.

What To Look For

The What To Look For questions, which appear on the Teacher's Guide pages, are a short list of what students should be able to do at the end of an investigation. Use the questions as you lead a class discussion, monitor small group activities, or quickly check student work. The Assessment pages for these lessons provide an overview of student work along with teachers' observations.

Skill Check

The Skill Check helps you plan homework in the upcoming phase and review essential skills. It also provides the solutions for the Skill Quiz, a one-page reproducible quiz for each phase that focuses on the specific skills introduced or practiced in that phase. Teachers' notes contain suggestions on ways you can use the assessment information you gather to inform instruction.

Assessment Rubric

The Assessment Rubric describes what student work might look like at each of four different levels. An Assessment Rubric is provided for each phase assessment and the unit assessment, where it is accompanied by student work and teachers' notes from the classroom. A reproducible of the Assessment Criteria, corresponding to level 3 of the Assessment Rubric, is also available for student use. A general assessment rubric is provided for evaluating portfolios, which are an optional part of the assessment system.

Reporting to Parents

Although not in itself an assessment tool, the Reporting to Parents page brings together the rich information gathered by the What To Look For, Assessment Rubric, and Skill Check tools, and provides guidance in assigning letter grades. If you need to assign one grade for the entire unit, the information gathered from the different assessment tools can be recorded in the Assessment Checklist, page A3, to help you maintain a balance between concepts, skills, and processes.

ASSESSMENT CHECKLIST

The Assessment Checklist is on Reproducible page R1. You can use it to record the information gathered about each student with the different assessment tools and to note your observations. You can also give students their own copy of the checklist that they can use to organize and reflect on their work for their portfolios.

I used a point system to keep track of student work. For the daily assignments I gave students 10 points if it was complete and correct. If the student was missing part of the assignment or had some errors, I gave only half credit (5 points). I scored the phase assessments at 40 points for a 4 on the rubric, 30 points for a 3, etc. I counted the skill checks as a regular assignment and transferred the percentage correct to points (100% = 10 points). □

My students wanted to use the Assessment Checklist as a way to keep track of their homework and classwork. I modified the checklist before copying it by changing the "Assessment" heading to "Due Date" and writing in the dates for key assignments and the final project. The revised checklist not only helped students who were absent to work at home, but served as a planning sheet for both me and my students. □

Gulliver's Worlds
ASSESSMENT CHECKLIST

Name: _____ Period: _____ Date: _____

Lesson	Assignment Description	Assessment	Notes
Pre-assessment	How big are things in Colossal City?		
Lesson 1	The Sizes of Things in Brobdingnag		
Lesson 2	A Life-Size Object in Brobdingnag		
Lesson 3	How Big Is "Little" Glumdalclitch?		
Lesson 4	Telling Tales in Brobdingnag		
Phase One Skill Check	Skill Quiz 1 & Homework 1–4		
Lesson 5	Sizing Up the Lilliputians		
Lesson 6	Glum-gluffs and Mum-gluffs		
Lesson 7	Housing and Feeding Gulliver		
Lesson 8	Seeing Through Lilliputian Eyes		
Phase Two Skill Check	Skill Quiz 2 & Homework 5–8		
Lesson 9	Lands of the Large		
Lesson 10	Lands of the Little		
Lesson 11	Gulliver's Worlds Cubed		
Lesson 12	Stepping into Gulliver's Worlds		
Phase Three Skill Check	Skill Quiz 3 & Homework 9–12		
Post-assessment	How big are things in the land you chose?		

Comments:

Assessment

I found that my students fell into two groups: those that were rescaling using area measurements and those who used only linear measurement. The class had a good debate about whether the large stamp was 3 times as large or 9 times as large as the small one. For the moment, I left this debate unresolved. I noted that I should return to this debate when we later consider the effect of rescaling on length (1 dimension) versus area (2 dimensions) versus volume (3 dimensions). □

I had my students reflect on how they solved the problem of rescaling by asking the following questions:
- *How did you identify the basic information needed to solve the problem?*
- *What strategy did you use to solve the problem?*
- *How did you use reasoning or logic to make decisions throughout the problem? □*

WHAT TO LOOK FOR

Pre-assessment

You can use the Pre-assessment on page 277E of the Teacher's Guide to assess the prerequisites for the unit. At the end of the unit, you can compare this task to the final project to note growth that has occurred in the course of the unit. (See Post-assessment, page A17.)

DO STUDENTS' PRE-ASSESSMENTS DEMONSTRATE THE PREREQUISITES OF:

- measurement of lengths using units from U.S. customary and metric systems?

- measurement of lengths using fractions of units from U.S. customary and metric systems?

- conversion of units within a measurement system?

First, I measured both of the stamps in inches and then in centimeters. I then measured the distance in inches and then in centimeters. After that, I figured the difference between the length of the stamp and the length of the postcard. Once I found the differences in both units, I added that to the length of the stamp from Colossal City. In inches, the postcard was 7 7/16 inches by 7 13/16 inches. In centimeters, the postcard was 18 1/2 centimeters by 20 centimeters.

postcard lengths- 15cm by 11cm + 5 13/16 in by 4 7/16 in.

```
  4 1/2 "        4 13/16 "
+ 2 15/16       + 3
---------      ---------
  7 7/16 "       7 13/16 " = measurement in inches
```

```
  8 cm          11 1/2 cm
+12 1/2 cm      + 7     cm
---------      ----------
 20 1/2 cm      18 1/2 cm = measurement in centimeters
```

Our stamp is 1 inch by 1 1/2 inch & the envelope is 5.75 inches by 4 1/2 inches. Then you find the area of the envelope by going 5.75 x 4.5 = 26.375. Next the area of stamp by going 1 x 1.5 = 1.5. Then you subtract 1.5 from 26.= 25. which is the area of envelope with nothing on it. Next you make an equation to find out how many stamps can fit on the envelope, the equation is 1.5 x = 24.375. Then you divide them and 16.25 stamps can fit on the envelope. Now the size of the other stamp is 3" by 4 1/2". Then we find the area by going 3 x 4.5 which is 14. Then you multiply 16 x 14 = 224. which is the area of the envelope. The envelope is 16" by 14".

I know that there are two cm in one inch. So I you go 14 x 2 = 28 cm and then 16 x 2 = 32 cm and the envelope is 32 cm by 28 cm.

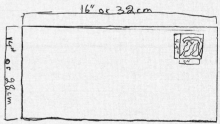

16" or 32cm

Phase One: Lessons 1, 2 & 3

The student work from Lessons 1, 2, and 3 of this phase should show an increased understanding of accurate measurement and appropriate size estimation, as well as scale and proportional relationships. One common error to look for in student work is that students may measure the original object without sufficient precision, perhaps by rounding to the nearest inch. Small errors in the original measures become large errors in the rescaled object.

I found that many of my students would measure an Ourland object in inches and then use feet to estimate the same object in Brobding-nag. The problem would come when they would use the scale factor to check their estimates and forget to convert to like units. I reminded my students that you can't compare apples and oranges (i.e., inches and feet) in a ratio. This really helped when we started to move between measurement systems in the second phase. □

I chose number one; that is 'A tree out side my home' And I want to know how tall is a tree that is out side my home. First I thought one way.

One way is that I know that I 4 feet 10 inches. So I went out side with my sister. I stood in front of the tree. And my sister said I am about ¼ of the tree. So I did 4 feet 10 inches times 4. That equals 232. And it is about 19 feet 4 inches.

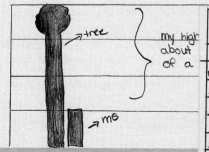

→tree

my high about ¼ of a

→me

Brobdingnang Penny

First I measured the diameter of a penny in Ourland and it equaled to 3/4 of a inch. Then I multiplied 3/4 × 12/1 because we found out that things in Brobdingnang are 12 × the size in Ourland.

3/4 × 12/1 = 36/4 = 9 in.

I marked 9 in on the diameter of the ... I marked 9 in ... st of all, I took the ... f the penny and ... 1/2 inches out and I drew in the rest.

Sometimes my students rescaled one dimension of the object very carefully and accurately, but then just estimated and sketched the other dimension. Often, it was obvious to others that the shape of the object had not been maintained accurately in rescaling—the rescaling activity had a nice self-checking quality to it. □

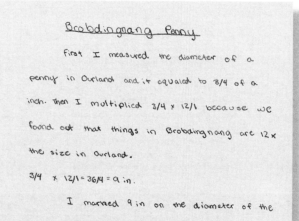

object	Brobdingnag scale size	Ourland actual size
table	30 feet tall	2.5 feet tall
meat dish	24 feet across	2 feet across
stalk of wheat	18 feet high	1.5 feet high
steps	6 feet high	½ feet high
giant	tall as ships mast	0.
giant's stride	ten yards	0.83 yards
door	96 feet tall	8 feet tall
bookshelf	72 feet long	6 feet long
chair	36 feet tall	3 feet tall
sofa	84 feet long	7 feet long

Many of the assignments in this phase could be checked by other students. I had students create a class chart to correct Lesson 1 and had them check the measurements of each other's drawings in Lesson 2. I collected Lesson 3 for their portfolio because I wanted to make sure they could compare it to a similar problem-solving activity involving volume in Lesson 7. □

GULLIVER'S WORLDS
Assessment

Some students showed a good understanding of scale and the importance of accurate measurements. If the student was also able to show in the labeled sketches a consistent use of scale factor using a variety of measurement units and a clear description of strategies, I gave their assignment a 4 on the rubric, because it went beyond the required three objects and described the area relationships between different objects within the story. □

I gave students a 3 if they were able to accurately rescale three objects using linear measurements and a scale factor. Sometimes sketches were accurate, but did not describe all the dimensions of an object. □

Somes students gave incorrect estimates of sizes in Brobdingnag. They simply knew that things were large, but did not use mathematics to determine how large. They described things to be much larger than 10 or 12 times the size of things in Ourland. I gave these papers a 2 because although key concepts were missed, all steps of the assignment were completed. □

4 3 2 1 ASSESSMENT RUBRIC
Phase One: Lesson 4

For this embedded assessment in Lesson 4, Telling Tales in Brobdingnag, students applied what they had learned in Phase One to write a story set in Brobdingnag and then summarize the methods they used to determine the measurements of objects in the story. The Assessment Rubric on the opposite page is designed to help you evaluate student work. See Reproducible page R5 for a version of the level 3 assessment criteria worded for student use.

A Walk on the Brob Side

I was walking alone one of Brobdingnag's huge sidewalks which was like walking in a gigantic Logan Airport. Suddenly I bumped into something. It was a quarter full Pepsi can four feet two inches, up to my chest. Then I figured out a way to get by it, somehow, and found myself stuck on a piece of bubble gum bigger than my foot! I was about to step and I saw a 2 ft. 6 in. long, 5 inches high log. What was it? A cigarette! My, does this place have litter!

Then I saw a big hand about 5 feet 9 in bend down and pick it up. I hope he did not notice me. Gosh, I felt so little! Well...... I WAS LITTLE! I started to run toward the cubbies, planning on hiding in someone's lunch bag. It took me about an our to get to a cubbie. Now was the hard part climbing into the bag! It was ab[...]
It was not a fence post but Ja[...]
way I found that out was she s[...]
it in an 11' 2" workbook. At fir[...]
she might drop the pencil, but [...]
she was used to a pencil of tha[...]

Hansi's Travels

I was walking along on the giant shelf I was on. It was about 75 feet high. Then I fell off onto the bed. It was 20 feet high. The pillow was enormous. It was 7 feet wide. After a while I found my way to the kitchen. There was a pencil 4 feet tall. Eventually I found my way to the dining room. There was a 8 foot long plate. I found a way out of the house [...]p. When I awoke I was [...] people. Later on I was to [...]e would continue.
      End

Brobdingnag Story

it was a pencil and they used it for writing the next thing I saw looked like a mattres but simply I know that i was an eraser. the next thing I saw looked like a piece of wood but it was realy just a ruler and then I said to my self everying is ten times the size as the stuff I youse.

            The end

Does student work...

- create a cohesive story that goes beyond the requirements of the assignment?

- communicate clearly and in detail the methods used to estimate, measure, and rescale?

- determine scale with no mathematical errors?

- include a precise and sophisticated list, table, or drawing comparing scale?

- create a cohesive story that meets the requirements of the assignment?

- communicate clearly the methods used to estimate, measure, and rescale?

- determine scale with no significant mathematical errors?

- include an accurate and complete list, table, or drawing comparing scale?

- create a story that meets most of the requirements of the assignment?

- communicate the methods used to estimate, measure, and rescale?

- determine scale with minor mathematical errors?

- include an incomplete list, table, or drawing comparing scale?

- create an incomplete or illegible story?

- communicate methods to rescale that miss key concepts of scale?

- determine scale with major mathematical errors?

- not include a list, table, or drawing comparing scale?

 **Goes beyond expectations**

 **Meets all expectations**

 Meets some expectations

 Falls below expectations

Assessment

My students had trouble converting between measurement units and reducing fractions and ratios, so I had them make up practice sheets for a partner based on the homework and skill quiz problems they missed. This way each pair had a custom-made piece of homework. I reminded students that there would be another quiz at the end of Phase Two that would measure their growth in these practice areas. ☐

SKILL CHECK

Phase One: Homework & Quiz

Students' conceptual understanding in Phase One is monitored daily using the **What To Look For** and evaluated using the **Assessment Rubric**. The lesson homework and the **Phase One Skill Quiz** are tools to check skill proficiency.

Homework

Homework for Lessons 1–4 appears in the Student Guide on pages 308–311. Depending on the needs of your students, you may assign all or part of the homework for each lesson. You may want to take students' homework performance into consideration as part of the overall phase evaluation.

Skill Quiz

The Phase One Skill Quiz is provided on Reproducible page R2. Solutions are given here. Hot Topics for Phase One are:

- Fractions and Equivalent Fractions
- Comparing and Ordering Fractions
- Size and Scale
- Area

SKILL QUIZ ANSWERS

1. 18 in.; $1\frac{1}{2}$ ft

2. 2 ft; $\frac{2}{3}$ yd

3. $\frac{1}{9}$ yd; 4 in.

4. $\frac{1}{3}$

5. $\frac{1}{8}$

6. $\frac{8}{15}$

7. $\frac{1}{3}$

8. 2:1

9. 4:1

10. 3:1

11. 10:1

12. 2:1

The student work from Lessons 5, 6, and 7 should show an increased understanding of measurement systems and the relationships among measurement units. They should also show a growing understanding of length, area, and volume. One common error to look for in student work is that students may not consider the appropriate number of dimensions for a problem, especially when three dimensions are required.

I noticed that, because the scale factor for both Brobdingnag and Lilliput was 12:1, some students were using the 1 inch equals 1 foot rule to rescale without any calculations. It became very clear in Lesson 6, when students had to use mum-gluffs and the metric system to rescale, who could actually calculate measurements using a scale factor. □

You may want to check students' writing to make sure that they are consistently applying a scale factor that reduces the size of the original object and are measuring with appropriate levels of precision for the task. In addition, students should be able to apply the concept of mean, median, or mode in solving problems. □

1:12	Ourland	Lilliput
man	6' tall	6" tall
trees	10' tall	10" tall
sheep	3' tall	3" tall
cows	6' tall	6" tall
student	5' tall	5" tall
your age	5' tall	5" tall
footprint	8" tall	1½" tall
handprint	6" tall	2½" tall

Math
Lesson 7

Mattress	Ourland	Lilliput
Mattress	18 sq ft	1.5 sq ft / 18 sq in
Length - 6 feet - 72 inches		Length - 6 inches
Width - 3 feet - 36 inches		Width - 3 inches

3 ft

144 mattresses

6 goes into 72 12 times, 3 goes into 36 12 times. 12 × 12 = 144 mattresses, 144 Lilliputian mattresses would fit on one from my land. I think this is logical.

...t just 12 ...sses would

Lesson 7

1 in width   ...in Length   1½ in Height

Ourland T.V.
Height = 1½ ft
Length = 2 ft
Width = 1 ft

Assessment

One assignment not only described more than three objects, but made comparisons between Ourland and Lilliput in area and volume. The story was interesting and included the humorous aside of Gulliver not being able to find the bones in the Lilliputian turkey. I gave this paper a 4 because I was able to visualize this world in 3 dimensions from the accurate descriptions. ☐

Although it is a well-written story with dialogue discussing sizes, I gave Angel's paper a 3 because the objects are compared using only two dimensions. He does an excellent job of incorporating non-standard measurement when he has the captain of the 2-foot ship describe how a shark bit off 2 mum-gluffs of his leg, but some of the conversions between systems are incorrect. ☐

I gave Usha's paper a 2 because of mathematical errors in rescaling linear measurements. The story is clear, and it is obvious that time was spent on the task, but the linear and area relationships between Lilliput and Ourland are inaccurate. ☐

Phase Two: Lesson 8

In Lesson 8, Seeing Through Lilliputian Eyes, students applied what they had learned in Phase Two to write a story comparing the volume and area of various Lilliputian objects to the same objects in Ourland. Students can compare their writing from this assessment with the writing from the Phase One assessment to see their growth. See Reproducible page R6 for a version of the level 3 assessment criteria worded for student use.

My Dinner with the King and Queen

I was invited to a feast with the King and Queen of Lilliput, although for me it was not exactly a feast. The top of their table was about as big as the top of a shoebox (14 feet long and 6 feet wide). I had to sit on the floor. The plates were about the size of m[ ] (1/2 inch). We each had a whole roa[ ] chicken on our plate, but it was only [ ] size of an almond to me. It was har[ ] the bones in the chicken, so I just cr[ ] them up and didn't feel a thing.

I told the king that a mum-gluf[ ] as big as an inch in Ourland, and that [ ] was considered to be really small. H[ ] amazed.

"What sort of things in your lan[ ] a mum-gluff long" the Queen asked.

"Some coins, a paper clip and a mum-gluff." I said.

"Wow" said the King.

I was still hungry after dinner, [ ] okay.

Gullivers World

A DAY AT A VERY BIG BEACH!

One day when I was at home I got kind of bored so I decided to go to the beach. While I was walking on the beach I saw a rock 2 cm high and 2½ cm wide. It was as big as a pebble in Ourland! I remembered that I had a pebble in my pocket, so I took it out and it was almost the same size. As I was walking I discovered lots of things. It was such an adventure to see creatures on the beach. When I was looking around I saw a lilliputian and had a conversation with one this is how it started: "Why hello" I said. "Hello". Everything is so different in Lilliput from Ourland!

Lesson 8

My Conversation with Lilliputians

Hi, I'm in Lilliput with a Lilliputian man. We are walking down main street, and looking into all the stores.

a furniture store[ ] were TV's 5 cm wide [ ] 5 cm long. There was [ ] wide, 4 cm tall, and [ ] the lilliputian man [ ] to his house which [ ] tall, 60 cm long, and [ ] Of course I couldn't [ ] stood outside looking [ ]ery. There was a three [ ] cm wide. He came out again [ ] would have to walk home.

Does student work...

- portray a creative and cohesive story that goes beyond the requirements of the assignment?
- communicate measurements using different systems, with conversions between systems?
- rescale linear measurements with accurate computations?
- compare area and volume relationships?
- describe in detail estimation and measurement strategies?

- portray a cohesive story that meets the requirements of the assignment?
- communicate measurements using different systems?
- rescale linear measurements with accurate computations?
- compare area relationships?
- describe clearly estimation and measurement strategies?

- create a story that meets most of the requirements of the assignment?
- communicate measurements using one system?
- rescale linear measurements with minor mathematical errors?
- describe briefly of the methods used to estimate, measure, and rescale?

- create an incomplete or illegible story?
- not communicate a description of measurement systems?
- rescale linear measurements with major mathematical errors?
- include an explanation that misses key concepts of scale?

 Goes beyond expectations

 Meets all expectations

 Meets some expectations

 **Falls below expectations**

I wanted my students to be comfortable using the metric system without having them worry about converting between the U.S. customary system and the metric system. I built on their knowledge of base 10 systems and provided additional practice working with metric units in a ratio before giving them the skill quiz. ☐

Students' conceptual understanding in Phase Two is monitored daily using the **What To Look For** and evaluated using the **Assessment Rubric**. The lesson homework and the **Phase Two Skill Quiz** are tools to check skill proficiency.

Homework

Homework for Lessons 5–8 appears in the Student Guide on pages 312–315. Depending on the needs of your students, you may assign all or part of the homework for each lesson. You may want to take student's homework performance into consideration as part of the overall phase evaluation.

Skill Quiz

The Phase Two Skill Quiz is provided on Reproducible page R3. Solutions are given here. Hot Topics for Phase Two are:

- Size and Scale

- Systems of Measurement

- Volume

- Addition and Subtraction of Fractions

- Multiplication and Division of Fractions

SKILL QUIZ ANSWERS

1. $\frac{1}{10}$

2. $\frac{64}{100}$

3. $\frac{967}{1,000}$

4. $\frac{4}{1,000}$

5. $\frac{3}{1,000,000}$

6. 100 cm

7. 5 cm

8. 2,000 m

9. 0.004 m

10. 3,000 cm

11. $\frac{240 \text{ mm}}{24 \text{ mm}}$; 1:0.1, or 10:1

12. $\frac{300,000 \text{ cm}}{3 \text{ cm}}$; 1:0.00001, or 100,000:1

Phase Three: Lessons 9, 10 & 11

The student work from Lessons 9, 10, and 11 of this phase should show an increased understanding of volume as well as noninteger scale and proportional relationships. One common error to look for in students' work is that students may not accurately convert between fractions and decimals as they calculate scale factors.

Because this phase culminated in a museum, I decided to have students post their work around the room as each lesson was completed. I would have them check the work with me or another student to make sure it was correct before they posted the work. I found that the most common errors were inaccurate calculations of scale factors that often involved a forgotten decimal or a need to convert to like units. □

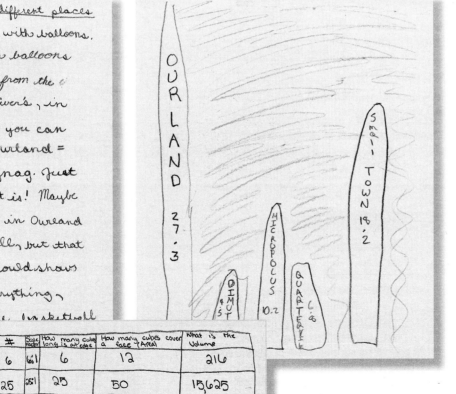

6 Different faces, from all different places

This display was made with balloons. The reason I made it with balloons was to show people's faces from the 6 different lands of Gulliver's, in 3-D image. From that you can see 144 faces from Ourland = 1 face from Brobdingnag. Just imagine how big that is! Maybe you're confused because in Ourland our heads are very small, but that was shrunk down so I could show the same scale and everything, but not use up a whole basketball court for a Brobding

#	Scale Factor	How many cubes long is an edge	How many cubes cover a face (Area)	What is the Volume
6	6:1	6	12	216
25	25:1	25	50	15,625
100	100:1	100	200	1,000,000
2.5	2.5:1	2.5	5	15.625

Assessment

Phase Three: Lesson 12

I gave one group's display a 4 because the students in this group created their own world based on area and volume relationships. The model of a small girl fit comfortably in the back seat of the model car, while the sky scraper and department store were in proportion with doors and windows that were to scale. Every detail was correct, right down to the parking places and the stripes on the road. □

Some students determined the scale factor of existing doll furniture to Ourland and then created additional furniture and people to scale. I gave the display a 3, for although the models were rescaled correctly, the house that the group constructed around the furniture was not in proportion. □

If a display was very creative, but the one of the models was not rescaled correctly and the other was not in proportion, I gave it a 2 and asked the students to check their measurements. □

In Lesson 12, Stepping Into Gulliver's Worlds, students applied what they had learned in the unit to a final project: designing a display that accurately uses scale to create one of the worlds Gulliver visited. The Assessment Rubric in the opposite page is designed to help you evaluate student work. See Reproducible page R6 for a version of the level 3 assessment criteria worded for student use.

This is a little girl that is about 3 cm high. She is about 1 cm in width. The name of the city... She... Fits... faci... 40:... hou... ulo... son... our... 120 c...

how tall she is in her land, (3 cm) into how tall she is in our land, (120 cm) and I got 40. So that makes the girl the right size.

Does student work...

- create an imaginative and cohesive display that goes beyond the requirements of the assignment?

- compare the sizes of objects/ people in all three dimensions, with an emphasis on volume and area relationships?

- determine scale of objects/ people with no estimation or mathematical errors?

- describe linear, area, and volume measurements of objects using exponents?

- communicate a sophisticated understanding of scale?

- create an imaginative and cohesive display that meets the requirements of the assignment?

- compare the sizes of objects/ people in all three dimensions?

- determine scale of objects/ people with no significant estimation or mathematical errors?

- describe linear, area, and volume measurements of objects using standard measurements and comparisons?

- communicate a clear understanding of scale?

- create a display that meets most of the requirements of the assignment?

- determine scale of objects/ people with minor estimation or mathematical errors?

- describe linear, area, or volume measurements of objects using comparisons only?

- communicate a basic understanding of scale?

- create an incomplete or illegible display?

- determine scale of objects/ people with major estimation or mathematical errors?

- describe measurements in one dimension only?

- show major misconceptions in understanding of scale?

 Goes beyond expectations

 Meets all expectations

 **Meets some expectations**

 **Falls below expectations**

Assessment

Phase Three: Homework & Quiz

For some of my students this phase was the first time they had used exponents with measurement units. I took some extra time with the centimeter cubes and let them practice covering two-dimensional objects to find the area in square centimeters and filling three-dimensional objects to find the volume in cubic centimeters. □

Students' conceptual understanding in **Phase Three** is monitored daily using the **What To Look For** and evaluated using the **Assessment Rubric. The lesson homework and the Phase Three Skill Quiz are tools to check skill proficiency.**

Homework

Homework for Lessons 9–12 appears in the Stuent Guide on pages 316–319. Depending on the needs of your students, you may assign all or part of the homework for each lesson. You may want to take homework performance into consideration as part of the overall phase evaluation.

Skill Quiz

The Phase Three Skill Quiz is provided on Reproducible page R4. Solutions are given here. Hot Topics for Phase Three are:

- Fraction, Decimal, and Percent Relationships
- Size and Scale
- Length and Distance
- Area

SKILL QUIZ ANSWERS

1. 0.5
2. 0.25
3. 0.67
4. 0.2
5. 0.125
6. $5 \times 5 \times 5 = 125$
7. $8 \times 8 = 64$
8. $4 \times 4 \times 4 = 64$
9. $7 \times 7 = 49$
10. $5 + 5 + 5 + 5 = 20$ cm
11. $5 \times 5 = 25$ cm^2
12. 20 cm, 20 cm; $4 \times 20 = 80$ cm, $20 \times 20 = 400$ cm^2

Post-assessment

I had my students reflect on their growth in problem solving by answering the following questions and comparing their answers and work to the pre-assessment:

- *How did I identify the basic information needed to solve the problem?*
- *What strategy did I use to solve the problem?*
- *How did I use reasoning or logic to make decisions throughout the problem?* □

To get a sense of your students' growth over the course of the unit, you can compare students' pre-assessment work (see page A4) with their work from Lesson 12. Ask students to compare their pre-assessment estimates of linear measurements to their Lesson 12 investigations involving area and volume relationships. Students should reflect on the tools they used to solve the problem first in the Pre-assessment and then in Lesson 12.

I noticed that most students were now using accurate calculations to compare linear and area measurements. I also noticed that students now had sophisticated strategies to rescale objects using nonintegers and standard and nonstandard measurements, and they could articulate the relationship between rescaling and area and volume. □

DID STUDENTS DEMONSTRATE GROWTH IN:

- rescaling using integer and noninteger scale factors?
- comparing and analyzing size relationships among several lands?
- developing strategies for predicting the sizes of objects in different lands?
- creating accurate scale models and scale drawings?
- comparing the effects of rescaling on linear, area, and volume measurements?
- describing measurements using different systems and exponents?
- communicating mathematical information with diagrams and words?
- using measurement and estimation to determine length, width, and height of an object?

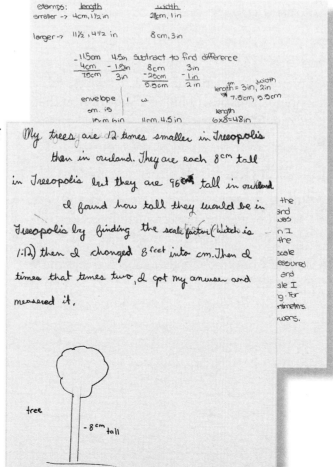

Assessment

I wanted my students' portfolios to show their growth in the three areas of skills, concepts, and problem solving. As a class, we brainstormed what were the "big ideas" of the unit, and made a list of all the skills and concepts they had learned in the unit. Next, we made a list of ways students had used writing to solve problems or explain something. I had students choose two pieces from each category (skills, concepts, and problem solving) that showed growth and include their final project. When everyone had made their choices, I had them write me a letter explaining why they had chosen certain things, and I had them evaluate their portfolios on a scale of 1–4 (4 being lots of growth, 1 being not much growth). I told students that their portfolio would be only part of their final unit grade. □

Portfolio Review

The focus of the portfolio evaluation is to gain insight into students' growth over time and to see how they view themselves as mathematicians. The portfolio should show students' increasing ability to communicate mathematically, solve problems, and make mathematical connections. The Assessment Rubric on the opposite page is designed to help you evaluate student work. See Reproducible page R7 for a version of the level 3 assessment criteria worded for student use.

FOR THIS UNIT THE FOLLOWING ITEMS WORK ESPECIALLY WELL TO SUPPLEMENT A STUDENT'S BASIC PORTFOLIO:

- a photo or a sketch of the student's work with manipulatives or a photo of a large project that will not fit in the portfolio

- an entry from the student's daily journal

- a student's letter to the reader describing each item

- a report of a group project, including a description of how the student contributed

- student work from another subject area using mathematics

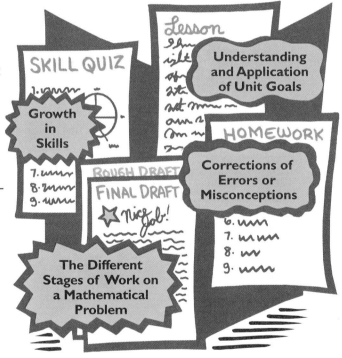

Does the portfolio show...

- significant mathematical growth in understanding and application of unit goals?

- significant mathematical growth in skill development?

- creativity and quality of work that go beyond the assignment?

- timely completion of assignments?

- no significant mathematical errors in assigned work?

- clear, coherent, and thoughtful explanations of mathematical process?

- some mathematical growth in understanding and application of unit goals?

- some mathematical growth in skill development?

- acceptable quality of work?

- timely completion of assignments?

- no significant mathematical errors in assigned work?

- clear explanations of mathematical process?

- understanding and application of unit goals?

- skill development that is documented with little growth?

- inconsistent quality of work?

- assignments that are complete but not always on time?

- minor mathematical errors in assigned work?

- unclear explanations of mathematical process?

- key points missed in understanding and application of unit goals?

- skill development that is not documented?

- consistently poor quality of work?

- assignments that are consistently late?

- significant mathematical errors in assigned work?

- no explanations of mathematical process?

 Goes beyond expectations

 Meets all expectations

 **Meets some expectations**

 Falls below expectations

Assessment

ASSESSMENT

I used the final project rubric as 50% of the unit grade and combined the phase assessments, homework, and daily work as another 25%. The remaining 25% was split between their grades on the skill quizzes, some traditional tests I gave, and their class participation (problem solving and cooperative group work). I explained to parents that the final projects represented concepts, skills, and problem solving. ☐

I used the final project rubric to come up with a unit rubric. I added things like homework being on time, phase-assessment scores, skill growth, and class participation. I then used this rubric to generate one score for the entire unit. I found that this way I could look at the displays (or the final application) and take into account the quality and quantity of the work that got the student to this point. I was also able to factor in student growth. ☐

Reporting to Parents

If you need to assign a single letter grade to reflect all the rich information students have gathered over the course of the unit, remember to maintain a balance between concepts, skills, and processes when doing so. In this particular unit, the final project is cumulative, and the rubric score from the project should be a large part of any grade given.

Skill Proficiency

By combining the Skill Checks, Homework and any Handbook assignments, you should be able to demonstrate to parents their child's ability to practice the skills involving calculation, estimation, measurement, and conversion beyond the contexts of the in-class investigations. Although skills in numbers, measurement, and geometry are an integral part of the daily lessons in this unit, Lesson 9, Lands of the Large, in which students repeatedly calculate scale factors using different measurements, is an obvious example to show parents how skills are incorporated into an investigation.

Conceptual Understanding

In this unit, the concepts covered in the embedded phase assessments for Phases One and Two are also incorporated into the final project at the end of Phase Three. As a result, parents can see their child's conceptual understanding of rescaling objects on a giant scale from Phase One, combined with the work with rescaling objects on a tiny scale in Phase Two, demonstrated in the

final project they produce in Lesson 12. You can also use Lesson 11, Gulliver's Worlds Cubed, as a specific example to demonstrate to parents how an investigation introduces geometric concepts that are an essential foundation for the study of geometry in high school.

Mathematical Processes

Problem solving and mathematical communication occur regularly in daily lessons. The final project is ideal for showing parents the nature of the problem-solving and mathematical communication processes in which their child is engaged. The problem situation of designing a display that is accurate and communicating about the display in writing and oral presentation are rich, real-world experiences for the student. You may want to invite parents to visit the class for a "Museum Tour" to see the students' completed final projects.

ANSWER KEY

LESSON 1, page 281
Compare Sizes to Determine a Scale Factor

1–3.

Object	Brobdingnag	Ourland
Stalk of wheat	About 18 feet	$1\frac{1}{2}$ feet
Stone step	6 feet high	6 inches
Man	As tall as mast of ship	Between 5'10" and 6'3"
Apple core	Like a log	$3\frac{1}{2}$ inches
Farmer's stride	10 yards	$2\frac{1}{2}$ feet
Meat dish	24 feet across	2 feet
Table	30 feet high	$2\frac{1}{2}$ feet
Cat	3 times the size of an ox	About 2 feet long
Desk (length)	24 feet	2 feet
Desk (height)	36 feet	3 feet
Desk (width)	30 feet	$2\frac{1}{2}$ feet
Crayon box (length)	4 feet 6 inches	$4\frac{1}{2}$ inches
Crayon box (width)	3 feet 6 inches	$3\frac{1}{2}$ inches
Crayon box (height)	8 inches	$\frac{2}{3}$ inch
Scissors (length)	5 feet	5 inches
Scissors (width)	3 feet	3 inches

LESSON 4 REPRODUCIBLE R20
Headlines

1. a. F
   b. F
   c. T
   d. T
   e. F
   f. T

LESSON 5, page 291
Create a Chart to Compare Sizes

1–2.

Object	Lilliput *	Ourland *
Man	6 inches	6 feet
Trees	7 feet	84 feet
Sheep	2 inches	2 feet high
Cows	4 inches	4 feet high
Student	$4\frac{1}{2}$ inches	$4\frac{1}{2}$ feet
Student handprint	$\frac{1}{2}$ inch	6 inches
Student footprint	$\frac{5}{8}$ inch	$7\frac{1}{2}$ inches
Average boy student	5 inches	5 feet
Average handprint	$\frac{3}{8}$ inch	$4\frac{1}{2}$ inches
Average footprint	$\frac{1}{2}$ inch	6 inches

*Answers will vary. Data for Lilliput and Ourland are based on a scale factor of 1:12.

LESSON 8 REPRODUCIBLE R21
Metric Headlines

1. a. F
   b. F
   c. F
   d. T
   e. F
   f. F
   g. T
   h. T

LESSON 9, pages 300–301
Investigate Proportions of Faces

Answers may vary depending on students' precision of measurement. For this investigation it may be helpful to have the whole class use the same measurement system—metric or standard. Scale factors should be close to the following:

Gargantua   7.5:1 (15:2)

Behemoth   4.5:1 (9:2)

Maximar   3:1

Upscale   1.5:1 (3:2)

Describe a Scale Factor for Brobdingnag

Items in Brobdingnag have dimensions that are 12 times those of the related items in Ourland. Starting with the ratios found previously for comparing to the sizes of objects in Ourland, the number 1 can be replaced by 12 on the right side of each ratio. Simplify where possible.

Gargantua   7.5:12 (5:8)

Behemoth   4.5:12 (3:8)

Maximar   3:12 (1:4)

Upscale   1.5:12 (1:8)

LESSON 10, page 303
Create a Table to Show Size Relationships

Ourland	Lilliput	Dimutia	Quarterville	Micropolis	Small Town
100 in.	8.3 in.	16.7 in.	25 in.	37.5 in.	67 in.
75 in.	6.25 in.	12.5 in.	18.75 in.	28.125 in.	50 in.
50 in.	4.17 in.	8.3 in.	12.5 in.	18.75 in.	33.3 in.
25 in.	2.08 in.	4.2 in.	6.25 in.	9.375 in.	16.67 in.
10 in.	0.83 in.	1.67 in.	2.5 in.	3.75 in.	6.7 in.

Write a Guide for Using the Table

Ourland, 80 in.; Lilliput, 6.67 in.; Dimutia, 13.33 in.; Quarterville, 20 in.; Micropolis, 30 in.; Small Town, 53.3 in.

Lilliput, 5 in.; Ourland, 60 in.

Small Town, 25 in.; Ourland, 37.5 in.; Lilliput, 3.125 in.; Dimutia, 6.25 in.; Quarterville, 9.375 in.; Micropolis, 14.06 in.

ADDITIONAL SOLUTIONS

LESSON 11, pages 304–305
Investigate Cube Sizes in Different Lands

Models of cubes at 2, 3, and 4

  2

 4

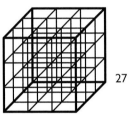 8

 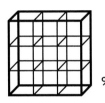 3

9

27

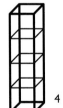 4

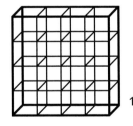 16

(not enough cubes) 64

Collect Data for Two and Three Dimensions

1. Measurement units may vary.

Scale Factor	How Many Cubes Long Is an Edge? (length)	How Many Cubes Cover a Face? (area)	How Many Cubes Fill the Cube? (volume)
2:1	2 cubes = 2 inches	4 cubes = 4 inches^2	8 cubes = 8 inches^3
3:1	3 cubes = 3 inches	9 cubes = 9 inches^2	27 cubes = 27 inches^3
4:1	4 cubes = 4 inches	16 cubes = 16 inches^2	64 cubes = 64 inches^3
5:1	5 cubes = 5 inches	25 cubes = 25 inches^2	125 cubes = 125 inches^3
10:1	10 cubes = 10 inches	100 cubes = 100 inches^2	1,000 cubes = 1,000 inches^3
25:1	25 cubes = 25 inches	625 cubes = 625 inches^2	15,625 cubes = 15,625 inches^3

2. 2.5:1   15.625 inches^3

   6:1   216 inches^3

   20:1   8,000 inches^3

   100:1   1,000,000 inches^3

Gulliver's Worlds
ASSESSMENT CHECKLIST

Name: _____ Period: _____ Date: _____

Lesson	Assignment Description	Assessment	Notes
Pre-assessment	How big are things in Colossal City?		
Lesson 1	The Sizes of Things in Brobdingnag		
Lesson 2	A Life-Size Object in Brobdingnag		
Lesson 3	How Big Is "Little" Glumdalclitch?		
Lesson 4	Telling Tales in Brobdingnag		
Phase One Skill Check	Skill Quiz 1 & Homework 1–4		
Lesson 5	Sizing Up the Lilliputians		
Lesson 6	Glum-gluffs and Mum-gluffs		
Lesson 7	Housing and Feeding Gulliver		
Lesson 8	Seeing Through Lilliputian Eyes		
Phase Two Skill Check	Skill Quiz 2 & Homework 5–8		
Lesson 9	Lands of the Large		
Lesson 10	Lands of the Little		
Lesson 11	Gulliver's Worlds Cubed		
Lesson 12	Stepping into Gulliver's Worlds		
Phase Three Skill Check	Skill Quiz 3 & Homework 9–12		
Post-assessment	How big are things in the land you chose?		

Comments:

PHASE ONE
Skill Quiz

Provide the missing equivalent measurements.

1. $\frac{1}{2}$ yd = _____ in. = _____ ft

2. 24 in. = _____ ft = _____ yd

3. $\frac{1}{3}$ ft = _____ yd = _____ in.

Reduce each fraction to the lowest terms.

4. $\frac{5}{15}$

5. $\frac{3}{24}$

6. $\frac{72}{135}$

7. $\frac{49}{147}$

Convert each ratio to like units and reduce it to the lowest terms to show the scale factor. HINT: In the final scale factor, one of the numbers in the ratio should be a 1.

8. $\frac{1}{2}$ ft:3 in.

9. 2 yd:18 in.

10. $1\frac{1}{4}$ yd:15 in.

11. 120 in:1 ft

12. $\frac{4}{9}$ yd:$\frac{2}{3}$ ft

PHASE TWO
Skill Quiz

Write the following decimals as fractions.

1. 0.1   **2.** 0.64

3. 0.967   **4.** 0.004

5. 0.000003

Supply the missing equivalent measurement.

6. 1 m = _____ cm

7. 50 mm = _____ cm

8. 2 km = _____ m

9. 0.4 cm = _____ m

10. 0.03 km = _____ cm

Convert these fractions to like measurement units and then reduce each fraction to its lowest terms. Make each fraction into a scale factor. HINT: In the final scale factor, one of the numbers in the ratio should be a 1.

11. $\dfrac{24 \text{ cm}}{24 \text{ mm}}$ **12.** $\dfrac{3 \text{ km}}{3 \text{ cm}}$

CENTIMETERS

PHASE THREE
Skill Quiz

Supply the equivalent decimal for each fraction.

1. $\frac{1}{2}$ **2.** $\frac{1}{4}$ **3.** $\frac{2}{3}$

4. $\frac{1}{5}$ **5.** $\frac{1}{8}$

Complete the chart by representing each exponent as an arithmetic expression and showing the value.

	Exponent	Arithmetic Expression	Value
6.	5^3		
7.	8^2		
8.	4^3		
9.	7^2		

5 cm

5 cm

10. What is the perimeter of the square? Describe how you found it.

11. What is the area of the square? Describe how you found it.

12. What would the length and width of the square be if the square above was enlarged by a scale factor of 4:1? How would you find the perimeter and area of the larger square?

PHASE ONE
Student Assessment Criteria

Does my work show that I can...

- create a complete story that meets the requirements of the assignment?

- clearly communicate how I estimated, measured and rescaled?

- figure out scale with no significant mathematical errors?

- include a correct and complete list, table, or drawing comparing scale?

Student Assessment Criteria

PHASE TWO

Does my work show that I can...

- write a complete story that meets the requirements of the assignment?
- clearly communicate measurements using different measurement systems?
- rescale linear measurements with correct computations?
- show a relationship between different areas?
- clearly describe estimation and measurement strategies?
- _____
- _____

PHASE THREE

Does my work show that I can...

- create a creative and complete display that meets the requirements of the assignment?
- compare the sizes of objects/people in all three dimensions?
- figure out scale of objects/people with no significant estimation or mathematical errors?
- describe linear, area, and volume measurements of objects, using standard measurements and comparisons?
- communicate a clear understanding of scale?
- _____
- _____

PORTFOLIO
Student Assessment Criteria

Does my portfolio show...

- that I have grown some in my understanding of math and in applying unit goals?

- that I have grown some in my math skills?

- that the quality of my work is acceptable?

- that I completed assignments on time?

- no major mathematical errors in assigned work?

- clear, well-written, and thoughtful explanations of my thinking?

-

-

-

Dear Family,

Our class will soon be starting a mathematics unit called *Gulliver's Worlds*. In this unit, students read and listen to journal entries based upon Jonathan Swift's classic book *Gulliver's Travels*, in which Gulliver visits Brobdingnag, the land of giants, and Lilliput, the land of tiny people. Using information from the journal entries, students learn about scale and proportion, different measurement systems, estimation, perimeter, area, and volume. The activities combine mathematics with reading, writing, and the visual arts.

Students will compare the sizes of things in Brobdingnag, Lilliput, and other lands to the sizes of things in "Ourland." For example, they meet a child from Brobdingnag who is almost 40 feet tall and they look for things around them—trees, telephone poles, and buildings—that are about as tall as the child. Students also learn how to make life-size drawings of objects from these lands.

The activities also invite students to write their own stories and create models of imaginary worlds where things are different sizes than they are in Ourland. Students use the language of mathematics to describe the sizes of people, animals, and things in these lands. Your child will have many interesting stories and discoveries to share with you.

You can help your child learn by playing "guess-timation" games in which you ask each other questions about the sizes of things. Encourage your child to come up with strategies to check these estimates. Here are some sample question to help you get started:

- About how many steps would it take you to walk to the end of the block? How many seconds would it take you?

- About how many times taller than you is that tree?

- How many objects can you find that are more than 1 foot long but less than 2 feet long?

- How many pieces of paper would it take to cover the entire table?

- Can you find an object that is about twice as long as another object? three times as long? four times as long?

- Can you find a rectangular object that is half the size of another object?

- About how many people could stand in this room? How many mattresses would it take to fill this room to the ceiling?

Exploring these kinds of questions about linear measurement, area, and volume helps children learn to use mathematics to understand the world around them.

Sincerely,

A Letter from Gulliver

The letter below is from Gulliver in Ourland. Look at the Colossal City stamp and figure out how big an envelope in Colossal City would be. Describe how you found your answer.

Gulliver's Journal

June 20, 1702

I, Lemuel Gulliver, hereby begin a journal of my adventures. This will not be a complete record, for I am not by nature the most faithful of writers. I do promise, however, to include any and all events of general interest.

The urge to visit strange and exotic lands has driven me since my youth, when I studied medicine in London. I often spent my spare time learning navigation and other parts of mathematics useful to travelers.

This spring I shipped out in the ship named Adventure under Captain John Nicholas. I had signed on as ship's doctor, and we were bound for Surat. We had a good voyage until we passed the Straits of Madagascar. There the winds blew strongly, and continued for the next twenty days. We were carried fifteen hundred miles to the east, farther than the oldest sailor aboard had ever been.

Lemuel Gulliver

August 29, 1702

We finally sighted land again today. Whether it was part of an island or continent I could not say. We went ashore near a small creek. While the sailors brought aboard water, I explored the countryside.

I was gone only a short time. Yet when I headed back toward the landing site, the sailors were already rowing frantically out to sea. No explanation was needed, for I could see a huge creature chasing them through the water. It stopped, though, at a sharp reef, and so the sailors escaped.

This was, I admit, of small comfort to me, because I was now alone. Fearing for my safety, I scampered inland. Beyond a steep hill, I discovered tall blades, about eighteen feet high. They appeared to be grass. I reached a stone stairway, but finding each step to rise six feet, I was unable to climb it. The trees along its edge were so tall I could not guess their height.

Such growth and size astounded me. Yet if I hoped to survive in this strange land, I realized I was going to have to learn the scale of things here and how they compared to things at home in England.

Lemuel Gulliver

Gulliver's Journal

August 29, 1702

I had not a moment to rest, as another monster was approaching. I now saw that in form he resembled a human being. It was his size—as tall as a ship's mast—that made him appear to be a monster. Scared and confused, I backed away, tripping over an apple core that lay like a log behind me. As I stood up again, the giant began cutting wheat with a great scythe. With every stride he traveled about ten yards closer to me, and I was faced with either being trampled on or cut in two. Therefore, I gave up my hiding place and shouted for his attention.

The giant stopped and looked about in confusion for some time. Finally, he spotted me. He picked me up gingerly between his thumb and forefinger and brought me within three yards of his eye. He blew my hair aside to get a better look at my face. He then put me down again on all fours. I stood up, however, to show him I was not an animal.

I pulled off my hat and bowed. The giant then spoke to me, but I could not understand his words, and his voice pierced my ears like thunder. At last he pulled out his handkerchief and motioned for me to lie down upon it. In this way he carried me home.

The giant's family—his wife, a son, a daughter, and a grandmother—were preparing for the midday meal. The one huge meat dish, perhaps twenty-four feet across, sat on a table top that was about thirty feet above the floor. What held my attention longest, though, was the family cat. It was three times the size of an ox. To my great relief, it took no interest in me at all.

As I was shown around the room, I could see the boy considering my virtues as a toy. The girl, about nine years old, had gentler intentions. She protected me from his pokes and pinches, thereby earning my friendship.

Lemuel Gulliver

Gulliver's Journal

August 30, 1702

In the whole of their country, which I learned they call "Brob-ding-nag," they had never seen nor heard of a creature like myself. Despite the fact that I was merely the size of a small rodent in their land, they quickly accepted that I was a person from another land and they treated me with great kindness and respect.

The giant's wife gave me a temporary home in her writing desk until more suitable lodgings could be arranged. The desk was littered with all kinds of objects that, at first, I did not recognize. Upon closer inspection, however, I was able to distinguish various writing materials and books.

In an effort to gain some much-needed privacy, I leaned two large envelopes against a stack of books that measured 10 foot high. Crawling under the envelopes, I had a spacious shelter from prying eyes and a measure of peace. I then made a roomy bed of a small diary with an abandoned eraser as my pillow. Looking around my improvised room, I quickly did a calculation in my head and determined a piece of note paper would be the ideal covering for my long-awaited nap. Unfortunately, at this great size the paper was like cardboard and left me longing for my wool blanket back home.

As I emerged from my room, I noticed that the kind woman had placed a cracker upon the desk. Obviously she had noted that I had eaten precious little at table, and had thoughtfully provided a more appropriate repast than the 3-foot egg I had been presented this morning. Indeed I was very hungry, but because the cracker was so thick, I was unable to bite off a piece and was forced to jump up and down on my meal before eating it.

Lemuel Gulliver

Gulliver's Journal

November 25, 1702

My first impression of the girl in the family proved to be correct. She was very good-natured, kind in spirit, and patient in teaching me her language. She was considered small for her age, being just under forty feet tall. Therefore I called her Glumdalclitch, which I learned means "Little Nurse" in her language. She called me Grildrig, meaning "Little Puppet."

Glumdalclitch took excellent care of me. She prepared food of a size that I could eat. She made me shirts from their softest linen, though I must admit they felt as coarse as a burlap bag. She also prepared a doll's cradle in her room for me to sleep in, which was far more comfortable than the desk drawer. She took me to her school one day, and I enjoyed visiting with her classmates and telling them about my country's customs, although I wasn't sure they believed that small creatures like myself could create such a complex society.

As the months passed, news of my existence spread. One day, Glumdalclitch's father was offered a large sum of money if he would show me as a sight on market day. A few days later I was taken in a box on a bumpy ride. My only comfort was that Glumdalclitch was brought along to take care of me. She explained that the marketplace was a glonglun away—about eighteen of our miles. We arrived at the Green Eagle Inn before nightfall. I slept poorly, though, imagining what lay ahead.

In my first performance the next morning, I was taken to the largest room in the inn. It was perhaps three hundred feet on each side. I was placed on a table in the middle, and the crowd was in a rough circle around me. I walked about as Glumdalclitch directed me. I drank from her thimble, waved my sword, and leapt about, making cartwheels and somersaults. As a finale, I juggled three peas, continuing to do so as I walked across a tightrope of sewing thread stretched between two wood spools. By day's end I had performed twelve times. I was the weariest I had ever been in my life.

Lemuel Gulliver

Gulliver's Journal

June 12, 1704

My master, finding great profit in my shows, toured with me throughout the kingdom. My crowning achievement was an appearance before the King and Queen. They enjoyed the show and were so interested in learning more about my homeland, that I was invited to remain as a royal guest. I was pleased to accept, my only request being that Glumdalclitch remain as my companion.

While residing in the royal palace, I found ways to accomplish things that at home never required a second thought. For example, the royal carpenters prepared a special book holder and ladder so that I could use the library. My size led to some frightening situations. One morning, I was sitting by the window when twenty giant wasps came flying into the room. They flew around my head, confusing me with the noise and threatening me with their stings. I killed four of them with my sword and drove the rest off.

As summer approached, the King and Queen made plans for all of us to visit the seashore. I, and all my belongings, fit in a traveling box which Glumdalclitch carried by a handle. I traveled comfortably, as the furniture, even a bed, was attached firmly to the floor of the box.

When we reached the sea, the King ordered a stop for us to have a picnic. After going out briefly, I returned to rest in my box, which had been placed on a hillside. Suddenly, there was a violent pull upon the box handle. Hearing the flapping of wings overhead, I realized that a huge sea bird had grabbed the handle and carried the box and me aloft. Then, without warning, I felt myself falling swiftly. The box splashed at last into the ocean, but fortunately floated on the surface.

I lost track of the hours, but eventually heard a noise on the roof. A sharp hook grabbed hold of my window, and the box was hoisted up out of the water. Within a few minutes, a hole was cut in its side, and a sailor of my own size poked his head through it. The captain of the ship that had found me enjoyed hearing of my adventure, but he clearly found my story unbelievable. His opinion changed, however, as I brought out a ring from the queen, and the stings of the giant wasps.

We arrived home two months later, and I was very glad to see my wife and family again.

Lemuel Gulliver

Gulliver's Journal

August 5, 1706

Having been condemned by nature and fortune to a restless life, I soon left my native country again. This time I took a post on the Antelope, a trading ship bound for the South Sea. We set sail from Bristol, England this past May 4th.

My duties as a ship's doctor have been few. The crew is well and we have had no accidents. I had been spending much time on deck—until a storm suddenly came upon us. Captain Pritchard informed me at dinner that we had been driven far off our course into uncharted waters.

The storm grew steadily worse, and the rough seas tossed the ship about like a child's toy. At last the ship sank on a reef, and I became separated from my companions. Pushed toward shore by the wind and tide, I fell exhausted upon the softest and shortest grass I had ever seen. But before I could examine it further, I fell into a deep sleep.

When I awoke, I found my arms and legs strongly fastened to the ground. Even my hair was tied down. My frustration gave way to surprise as I saw what creatures had done this. Hundreds of them were scattered on the ground around me. They looked like men in every way but one—they were a mere six inches tall. I realized rather abruptly that it was now my turn to feel like a giant.

The boldest little man now climbed upon my chest. Seeing my discomfort, he ordered my head and one arm released. He then made a long speech in a strange language, which I did not understand at all. When he finished, he started to get down. At the last moment he tripped on a wrinkle in my shirt. He would have fallen had I not caught him in my free hand.

This act earned me much good will. Tiny baskets of meat and bread were served, which I ate two or three at a time. The meat, whether mutton, beef, or ham, I could not identify by taste. The loaves of bread were so small I swallowed several with little chewing. My captors then brought forward wagons filled with cider barrels. Each barrel was the size of a tiny cup, and I emptied a dozen.

Lemuel Gulliver

Gulliver's Journal

September 5, 1706

I was soon taken to a spot just outside a city, a city whose walls were only $2\frac{1}{2}$ feet high. It had two principal streets, each five feet wide. There were many shops and markets, and the largest signs might have filled a square on one of our chessboards. It was market day, and farmers had gathered in town to sell their fruits and vegetables. They haggled and bargained over apples no bigger than marbles and bunches of carrots as small as my thumbnail.

Tutors soon taught me the language of Lilliput, as I learned the country was called. Quinbus Flestrin—Great Man-Mountain—was the name the Lilliputians gave me.

The city inhabitants, though wary of me at first, grew used to my presence. Sometimes on hot days they enjoyed resting in my cool, vast shadow. As the weeks passed, I too felt more comfortable. I took walks through woods where the tallest trees stood about seven feet high. The meadows were filled with wildflowers, looking far prettier than the finest oriental carpet. Wherever I visited, I learned to watch my step. In a place where sheep were about 2 inches high and the cows perhaps twice that, it was best to walk carefully.

One afternoon I happened across a country school yard. The children swarmed over me, begging me to play. I let them tumble through my hair and slide down my hand. One brave boy, about twelve years old, let me make a tracing of him under his schoolmaster's supervision. He lay down on my journal while I traced his outline with my quill. He then stamped his hand print and footprint on the paper.

The schoolmaster agreed to let me draw his outline as well, along with his spectacles and belt. Students then gave me a lunch box and other items to outline in my journal. Then, not wishing to disturb their lessons, I thanked the class for their kind attention and bid them all a fond farewell.

Lemuel Gulliver

Gulliver's Journal

October 5, 1706

Two months after my arrival in Lilliput, I was invited to a banquet with the King and Queen. The dinner was held outside their palace in the royal courtyard because even the grand ballroom was not big enough to hold me. The King and Queen sat on specially constructed raised platforms so that I could speak to them more directly.

During dinner, the King and Queen told stories about their country and people, and I told stories of mine. Amazed at what I said, the Queen asked "How could you ever build a school large enough if all the children are as big as you say? How could you ever grow enough food to feed them?" The King found it especially hard to believe that he, one of the tallest men in his land, would be no bigger than a child's doll in mine. He informed me that he was $8\frac{1}{2}$ glum-gluffs tall, and that the Queen was 6 glum-gluffs tall. When I inquired what a glum-gluff was, he replied that it was $1\frac{1}{20}$ of a mum-gluff. He then kindly agreed to have his steward mark the length of 1 glum-gluff in my journal.

—— 1 glum-gluff

At one point the King mentioned Lilliput's continuing troubles with the country of Blefescu. This warring nation had recently gathered a large fleet of ships on the far side of a wide channel. Observing his concern, I offered to repay the Lilliputian's many kindnesses by removing the threat of the Blefescu fleet.

The next morning I waded across the channel to Blefescu. There were fifty ships in their harbor, each about the size of a child's wagon. The inhabitants there, though they had heard news of me, were not prepared for a fight. The sailors on board jumped into the water, scurrying to shore. I ignored them, and pulled up the anchor cables, collecting them together. Once this was done, I simply pulled the ships back to Lilliput. There I was greeted as a hero. I must confess, though, that my actions caused me only the trouble of a mild swim.

Lemuel Gulliver

Gulliver's Journal

April 7, 1707

Although I tried over the winter months to continue my service to Lilliput, in certain matters I could not help being a burden. Three hundred tailors had worked many days making me clothes to replace my shipwrecked rags. My bedding was also no small matter. It required piling up many of their mattresses together. Even then my bed was still uncomfortable, and I often tossed and turned in my sleep.

Of more concern was keeping me fed. Preparing my meals kept 400 cooks busy every day. On my behalf every village delivered three steers and forty sheep each morning. In addition, I lost track of the slices of bread and mugs of cider it took to satisfy my appetite.

Considering the burden that my presence placed on the population, I decided to leave when the first good chance appeared. It was very helpful to me at this time that a damaged longboat washed up on shore. The Lilliputians had no use for such a vessel, and happily helped me repair it. Once this was done, I bid Lilliput a fond farewell, and rowed out to sea.

A passing clipper ship sighted me on my second day out, and I was soon on my way home to England. The captain, John Biddel, treated me with much kindness, and wished to hear my story. I told it to him quickly. He listened with care, yet I knew he thought me disturbed in the head.

I had some evidence to support my claims, some parting gifts the Lilliputians had given to me. I showed the captain two presents from the king—a full-length portrait and fifty purses of gold. He examined them at length, being most impressed with the tiny Lilliputian gold coins. However, he remained skeptical overall, thinking these things could be the work of a trained craftsman.

I was confident I could change his mind on this point, however. I promptly showed him the six small cows and two bulls, with an equal number of ewes and rams, that I also carried with me in a special box. He was truly amazed at the sight of these animals. This worthy gentleman, now convinced of my honesty, then suggested that I write down my story and share it with the world. That I followed his suggestion can plainly be seen by this narrative.

Lemuel Gulliver

Gulliver's Journal

May 1, 1707

Upon my safe arrival home, I was surprised to find yet another souvenir from Lilliput. A tiny scrap of paper, no larger than a piece of confetti, was caught in the seam of my pocket. At first I could not read the writing, but after using a magnifying glass, I made out the message.

It seems that when I first arrived in Lilliput, the King asked two Lilliputian officers to take an inventory of the items found in my pockets. Somehow their list found its way into my pocket. For your amusement, I have endeavored to copy word for word their descriptions.

1. One great piece of coarse cloth, large enough to be a carpet for your Majesty's chief Room of State.

2. A great bundle of white thin substances, folded one over another, about the bigness of three men, tied with a strong cable and marked with black figures, with every letter almost half as large as the palm of our hands.

3. A long pole from the back of which extended 20 shorter poles, resembling the palace railings.

4. Several round flat pieces of yellow and silver metal, of different bulk, some so large and heavy that my comrade and I could hardly lift them.

5. Some wonderful kind of globe-like engine, part silver and part transparent metal, with a loud noise like the sound of a water-mill, attached by a great silver chain.

Lemuel Gulliver

Headlines

1. Check which of the following headlines could be a true story about Gulliver's adventures in Brobdingnag and which ones would be considered unbelievable.

a. Man Swims with Whale-Sized Goldfish

b. Traveler Reads Book That's as Tall as a Two-Story Building

c. Shipwrecked Surgeon Dodges Fork the Size of Shovel

d. Five-Foot Mouse Scares Visitor

e. Man Rides on Butterfly's Back

f. Man Floats on Raft Made of 12 Pencils

2. How do you know?

a. Choose one statement that you said could be true and write about your reasoning. What information did you use?

b. Choose one statement you said was unbelievable. Write about how you figured out that it could not be true.

3. Write your own headlines. Write at least one headline about Brobdingnag that could be true and at least one that is unbelievable.

Metric Headlines

1. Check which of the following headlines could be a true story about Gulliver's adventures in Lilliput and which ones would be considered unbelievable.

a. I Saw a Lilliputian House That Was 15 cm Tall and 25 cm Wide

b. I Could Carry a Lilliputian Car in My Pocket

c. I Saw a Lilliputian House That Could Fit in My Lunch Box

d. I Saw a Lilliputian Elephant That Was 30 cm Tall

e. I Saw a Lilliputian Football Field That Was the Size of an Ourland Doormat

f. I Saw a Lilliputian Door That Was the Size of an Ourland Postage Stamp

g. I Could Grow Five Lilliputian Trees in My Window Box

h. I Saw a Lilliputian Mountain That Was 40 m Tall

2. How do you know?

a. Choose one statement that you said could be true and write about your reasoning. What information did you use?

b. Choose one statement you said was unbelievable. Write about how you figured out that it could not be true.

3. Write your own headlines. Write at least one headline about Lilliput that could be true and at least one that is unbelievable.

Creating a Display in

Name of Land you have chosen

By: _____

Scale factor to Ourland: _____

Follow these steps to plan your display:

1. Description of Objects in the Display: Create at least three objects in one, two or three dimensions that will be part of the display.

Object	Dimensions (1-D, 2-D, 3-D)	Measurements
1.		
2.		
3.		

2. Presentation: Write a short presentation that describes the measurements of the objects in the display and compares them to Ourland. Describe and label the area and volume of the objects.

_____

_____

3. Interactive: Write a short description of how the visitors to the museum can step into the display.

_____

_____

4. Writing: Include your writing and any graphs or charts that will help museum visitors to understand Gulliver's Worlds.

The Ourland Museum Comment Card

Please take the time to fill out the comment card. Rate the display you are observing by circling numbers on a scale of 1–10 (10 being very good) to see how well it answers the following questions:

- Does the display look life-size?

  1   2   3   4   5   6   7   8   9   10

- Are the objects in the display in proportion?

  1   2   3   4   5   6   7   8   9   10

- Does the presentation describe linear, area, and volume measurements of objects?

  1   2   3   4   5   6   7   8   9   10

- Does the presentation compare sizes to sizes in Ourland?

  1   2   3   4   5   6   7   8   9   10

What could be realistically added or changed to make the display more real or interactive?

INDEX

Change
representing, 20–27

Circle graph, 265

Classification
angle, 178–181
polygon, 176–177, 180–181, 198, 200, 174–175
polyhedron, 186–187, 190–191, 202, 204
prism, 188
proper and improper fractions, 122–123, 133, 138, 153
pyramid, 189
quadrilateral, 182–183, 201

Clustering, 219

Common denominator, 116
addition and subtraction of fractions, 119–121, 123–127, 152–155, 93G
comparing fractions, 111, 113–115, 150, 93G

Common factors, 97–99, 142, 143
greatest, 99, 143

Common multiples, 100–101, 144
least, 100–101, 144, 116

Comparison
additive and place value number systems, 66–67, 60–61
of coordinate patterns, 344–345, 362
of decimals, 214–215, 217, 258, 259, 208
different names for the same number, 64–65, 85, 113, 115, 122, 149, 153, 49H
of equivalent expressions, 334–335, 358, 321G
of experimental data, 22–27, 42–44, 3G
of fractions, 108, 110–112, 114–115, 148–150, 217, 259, 308, 93G, 107, 116
of integers, 244–245, 270
of isometric and orthogonal views, 163G, 164–165
of measurement systems, 292–293, 313
number words in different languages, 56–57, 82

of percents, 266, 268
properties of number systems, 54–55, 81
using scale factor, 280–281, 290–291, 308, 312, 278–279, 288–289, 298–299
of survey data, 16–19, 40–41,12
to order numbers in multiple forms, 217, 259

Concave polygon, 184

Congruent figures
as faces of regular polyhedrons, 186–189

Continuous data, 21

Coordinate plane, 340–341, 360
comparing number patterns, 344–345, 362, 321H, 338–339
describing a picture, 340–341, 360
graphing a number rule, 342–343, 361, 321H, 338–339
graphing progress over time, 20–21

Convex polygon, 184

Cubes, 96–97
for modeling addition, 248–249, 272, 243
for modeling subtraction, 252–253, 274

Customary measures. See Measurement

D

Data collection
experiment, 22–27, 42–44
sampling, 30–35, 45–47
survey, 5–11, 16–19

Decimals, 208–229, 256–264
adding, 220–221, 260, 207G–207H, 218
comparing, 214–215, 217, 258, 259, 208
dividing, 226–227, 263, 207H, 218
estimating products, 224, 219
fractions and, 210–213, 233, 256, 257, 312, 316, 319, 107
money and, 210, 256

multiplying, 222–225, 261, 262, 207H
on a number line, 216, 258, 259
ordering, 214–215, 217, 258, 259
percent and, 232, 238, 265, 268, 230
place value and, 212, 257, 208
repeating, 228, 264, 107, 209
rounding, 216, 259
scale and, 298
subtracting, 221, 260, 207H, 218
terminating, 228, 264, 107, 209
word names for, 312

Denominator, 126
common, 97–99, 142, 143

Dimensions, 96–97

Discount, 231

Distribution
frequency, 10–11, 38, 5

Division
decimal, 226–227, 263, 207H, 218
estimating quotients, 139, 160
factors and, 328–329, 356
fraction, 136–141, 159–161, 93H, 106
mixed number, 137–139, 159–160
and multiplication, 141, 161, 128–129
order of operations and, 102–104, 145, 146
to rename a fraction as a decimal, 228, 264
whole number, 102–105, 145, 146

Double bar graph, 16–19, 40–41
creating, 17, 19, 40, 41, 3G
interpreting, 16, 18, 40, 41, 13

E

Edge, 186–187, 202, 184

Egyptian number system, 78–79, 91, 71

Equal angles, 179, 184

Equations. See also Expressions; Proportion, 109, 145
for target numbers, 103, 145

Equilateral, 176–177, 198, 184

Equivalent
division problems, 226, 263

Equivalent expressions, 334–335, 358, 321G

Equivalent fractions, 108, 110–115, 148–150, 213, 315, 93G, 94–95, 116–117

Error analysis
decimal addition, 220
using a graph, 24–25, 43
scale drawing, 283, 302–303
size relationships, 286–287

Estimation. See also Prediction
area, 182–183, 201, 284–285, 294–295, 310, 314
using clustering, 219
to compare fractions, 107
by comparison to the known, 280–281, 290–291
decimal products, 224, 219
decimal sums, 119
fraction products, 134, 158
fraction quotients, 139, 160, 129
front-end, 219
length, 284–285, 310
for locating the decimal point in an answer, 224, 262, 218
using non-standard units, 284–285
percent, 234, 236, 266, 267, 230–231
using rounding, 219
visual, 24–25, 284–285, 294–295
volume, 284–285, 294–295, 304–307

Expanded notation, 54–55, 81, 51

Experimental probability, 29–35, 45–47, 3G, 28–29

Exponents, 70–79, 88–91
expressions with, 74–75, 88, 89, 304–305, 318
model for, 72–73
order of operations and, 102, 145
place-value systems and, 76–77, 90, 70–71

pictures on a coordinate plane, 340–341, 360
a story, 26–27, 44
survey data, 6–11, 16–17, 36–38, 3G, 12–13
from a table, 14–15, 23, 39
to compare patterns, 344–345, 362, 321H, 346–347

Graphing calculator, 3H, 49H, 227H, 321H, 93H

Greatest common factor, 99, 143, 95

Grouping
conventions for algebraic notation, 334
order of operations and, 102–104, 145, 146

Gulliver's Journal
while in Brobdingnag, 276, 278, 280, 282, 284, 286
while in Lilliput, 288, 290, 292, 294, 296

H

Hawaiian numbers and words, 57

Hexagon, 183, 201, 185

Homework, 36–47, 80–91, 142–161, 194–205, 256–275, 308–319, 354–365

I

Improper fraction, 112, 122–124, 126, 133, 138, 153–155, 117

Inequality
decimal, 217, 258, 259
fraction, 112, 114, 149, 150
integer, 244, 270

Integer, 242–255, 270–275
addition, 246–249, 254–255, 271, 272, 275, 207H, 242–243
handbook, 247, 249, 251, 253
order, 244–245, 270
subtraction, 250–255, 273–275

Inverse operations, 329, 334–335, 349, 350, 356, 363, 364, 117, 129

Inverse Property of Multiplication, 129

Inverse proportionality, 128

Irrational number, 209

Isometric drawing, 168–173, 195–197, 163G, 164–165, 185

L

Least common denominator, 114, 94–95

Least common multiple, 100–101, 114, 144, 150, 95, 116

Length
conversion among customary units, 308, 311
conversion among metric units, 313, 314
customary units of, 280–283, 290–293, 308–309
estimating, 284–287, 308, 310
metric units of, 292–293, 296–297
non-standard units of, 292–293
ordering metric measures, 313
scale and, 280–283, 290–293, 304–305, 318

Like denominators, 126, 94–95, 116

Line graph, 22–27, 42–44
creating, 22, 24, 42, 43
interpreting, 22–27, 42–44

Linear data, 21

Linear graph, 342–345, 361, 362

Lines
parallel, 176–177, 198

Logic
and statement accuracy, 286–287
true and false statements, 240, 269
truth tests, 324–325, 352

M

Magic square, 121, 152, 154

Math Background, 4–5, 12–13, 20–21, 28–29, 50–51, 60–61, 70–71, 94–95, 106–107, 116–117, 128–129, 164–165, 174–175, 184–185, 208–209, 218–219, 230–231, 242–243, 278–279, 288–289, 298–299, 322–323, 330–331, 338–339, 346–347

Math focus
adding parts and taking them away, 93
between the whole numbers, 93
Brobdingnag, 279
Chinese abacus, 61
computing with decimals, 207
decimals, 206
describing functions and properties of shapes, 175
describing patterns using graphs, 339
describing patterns using tables, 323
describing patterns using variables and expressions, 331
finding and extending patterns, 347
fractions in groups, 93
the integers, 207
lands of large and lands of little, 299
Lilliput, 289
measuring progress over time, 20
mystery device, 51
number power, 71
percents, 207
probability and sampling, 28
representing and analyzing data, 12
surveys and measures of central tendency, 5
visualizing and representing cube structures, 165
visualizing and representing polygons and polyhedrons, 185
the whole of it, 92

MathScape Online, 3, 3H, 49, 49H, 93, 93G, 93H, 163, 163G, 207, 207H, 277, 277H, 321, 321G

MathScape Online Self-Check Quizzes, 5, 13, 21, 29, 51, 61, 71, 95, 107, 117, 129, 165, 175, 185, 209, 219, 231, 243, 279, 289, 299, 323, 331, 339, 347

Mayan
numbers and words, 57, 49G, 71

Mean, 8–11, 37–38, 229, 290–291, 3G, 4

Measurement
angle, 178–179, 199
area, 158, 182–183, 201, 263, 284–287, 294–295, 310, 314, 278–279, 288–289, 298–299
comparing systems of, 292–293, 313
converting among customary units of length, 308, 311
converting among metric units of length, 313, 314
customary units of length, 280–283, 290–293, 308–309
fractional parts of units, 280–283, 300–301, 308, 106, 129
metric units of length, 259, 292–293, 296–297
nonstandard units, 292–293
ordering metric lengths, 313
perimeter, 182–183, 201
precision and, 282–283
rate, 20–27
rescaling, 280–283, 290–293, 300–301, 308, 309, 278–279, 288–289
time, 256
volume, 284–287, 294–295, 310, 314

Median, 8–11, 37, 38, 290–291, 4

Mental math, 104, 146

Metric measures. See Measurement

Mill, 256

Millicurie, 256

Millisecond, 256

Mixed numbers
improper fractions and, 122, 153, 117

grouping, 102, 145, 334
less than, 112, 149, 150, 217, 258, 259, 270
repeating digits, 228

T

Technology
graphing calculator, 3H, 49H, 277H, 321H, 93H
software, 49G, 163H
spreadsheet, 3G, 227G, 321G
MathScape Online, 3H, 49H, 93H, 163G, 207H, 277H, 321G

Temperature, 229, 244

Terminating decimals, 228, 264, 107, 209

Theoretical probability, 30–35, 45–47, 28–29

Three-dimensional figure.
See also Polyhedron
description of, 167
isometric drawing of, 168–173, 195–197, 163G, 164–165
orthogonal drawing of, 170–173, 196–197, 163G–163H, 164–165
patterns and, 326–327, 355
rescaling, 294–297, 304–305, 314–315, 318, 298–299
rotated views, 195
two-dimensional drawing of, 166–167, 194, 163G–163H, 164–165
visualize and build, 166–167, 164–165

Time, 256

Transformations
changing one polygon into another, 176–177, 198
rotation of three-dimensional figures, 168–169, 195

Trapezoid, 182–183, 201, 185

Trends, broken-line graphs and, 22–27, 42–44, 20–21

Triangle, 182–183, 201, 185

Two-dimensional figure.
See also Polygon
properties of, 174–183, 198–201, 174–175
rescaling, 283, 294–297, 304–305, 314–315, 318, 278–279, 298–299

Two-dimensional representation
isometric drawing, 168–173, 195–197, 163G, 164–165
orthogonal drawing, 170–173, 196–197, 163G–163H, 164–165
of a three-dimensional figure, 166–167, 194, 163G–163H, 164–165

U

Unlike denominators, 108–121, 123–127, 148–155, 116–117

V

Variables
conventions for algebraic notation and, 332, 334
describing patterns with, 330–337, 357–359, 346–347
patterns with two, 336–337, 359

Variation,
measures of, 4

Vertex (vertices), 186–187, 202, 185

Visual Glossary
edge, 187
equal angles, 179
equilateral, 177
face, 167
isometric drawing, 169
opposite angles, 181
orthogonal drawing, 171
parallel, 177
prism, 189
pyramid, 189
regular shapes, 181
right angles, 179
vertex, 187

Volume
estimation of, 284–285, 294–295, 310, 314
exponents and, 318
rescaling, 294–297, 304–305, 314–315, 318, 298–299

W

Whole numbers, 94–105, 142–146
factors of, 94–99, 142, 143
multiples of, 100–101, 144
operations with, 102–105, 145, 146
prime, 96–99, 142, 143

Word equation, 330

Work backward, to find a pattern, 327, 329, 349, 356, 363

X

x-axis, 340

x-coordinate, 340

Y

y-axis, 340

y-coordinate, 340

Z

Zero
as an exponent, 72–73, 88
as a base ten placeholder, 63
signed numbers and, 10

Zero pair, 252–253, 274, 243